AAT
Professional Diploma Synoptic Assessment

Pocket Notes

These Pocket Notes support study for the following AAT qualifications:
AAT Professional Diploma in Accounting – Level 4
AAT Level 4 Diploma in Business Skills
AAT Professional Diploma in Accounting at SCQF Level 8

British library cataloguing-in-publication data

A catalogue record for this book is available from the British Library.

Published by:
Kaplan Publishing UK
Unit 2 The Business Centre
Molly Millars Lane
Wokingham
Berkshire
RG41 2QZ

ISBN 978-1-78740-036-8

© Kaplan Financial Limited, 2017

Printed and bound in Great Britain.

This Product includes content from the International Ethics Standards Board for Accountants (IESBA), published by the International Federation of Accountants (IFAC) in 2015 and is used with permission of IFAC.

The text in this material and any others made available by any Kaplan Group company does not amount to advice on a particular matter and should not be taken as such. No reliance should be placed on the content as the basis for any investment or other decision or in connection with any advice given to third parties. Please consult your appropriate professional adviser as necessary. Kaplan Publishing Limited and all other Kaplan group companies expressly disclaim all liability to any person in respect of any losses or other claims, whether direct, indirect, incidental, consequential or otherwise arising in relation to the use of such materials.

All rights reserved. No part of this publication may be reproduced, stored in a retrieval system, or transmitted, in any form or by any means, electronic, mechanical, photocopying, recording or otherwise, without the prior written permission of Kaplan Publishing.

Financial Statements of Limited Companies

Contents

Spreadsheets | **Study Text chapter** | **Page Number**

		Study Text chapter	Page Number
Chapter 1	The accounting function	1	5
Chapter 2	The use of key financial reports	2	13
Chapter 3	Internal controls	3	17
Chapter 4	Internal controls in computerised systems	4	27
Chapter 5	Ratio analysis	5	35
Chapter 6	Fraud	6	43
Chapter 7	Improving the accounting system	7	47
Chapter 8	Ethics and sustainability	8	53
Chapter 9	Recap of key aspects of Financial Statements of Limited Companies	A1	61
Chapter 10	Recap of key aspects of Management Accounting: Budgeting	A2	75
Chapter 11	Recap of key aspects of Management Accounting: Decision and Control	A3	89
Index			I.1

Preface

These Pocket Notes contain the key things that you need to know for the exam, presented in a unique visual way that makes revision easy and effective.

Written by experienced lecturers and authors, these Pocket Notes break down content into manageable chunks to maximise your concentration.

Quality and accuracy are of the utmost importance to us so if you spot an error in any of our products, please send an email to mykaplanreporting@kaplan.com with full details, or follow the link to the feedback form in MyKaplan.

Our Quality Co-ordinator will work with our technical team to verify the error and take action to ensure it is corrected in future editions.

A guide to the assessment

A guide to the assessment

The assessment

Four units within the Professional Diploma in Accounting are mandatory. Of these, three are assessed individually in end of unit assessments, but this qualification also includes a synoptic assessment, sat towards the end of the qualification, which draws on and assesses knowledge and understanding from all four mandatory units:

Examination

Professional Diploma Synoptic Assessment is assessed by means of a computer based assessment. The CBA will last for 3 hours.

In any one assessment, students may not be assessed on all content, or on the full depth or breadth of a piece of content. The content assessed may change over time to ensure validity of assessment, but all assessment criteria will be tested over time.

Learning outcomes & weighting

Assessment objective	Weighting
A01 Demonstrate an understanding of the roles and responsibilities of the accounting function within an organisation and examine ways of preventing and detecting fraud and systemic weaknesses.	10%
A02 Evaluate budgetary reporting; its effectiveness in controlling and improving organisational performance	20%
A03 Evaluate an organisation's accounting control systems and procedures	15%
A04 Analyse an organisation's decision making and control using management accounting tools.	20%
A05 Analyse an organisation's decision making and control using ratio analysis.	20%
A06 Analyse the internal controls of an organisation and make recommendations	15%
Total	**100%**

Pass mark

To pass a unit assessment, students need to achieve a mark of 70% or more.

This unit contributes 35% of the total amount required for the Professional Diploma in Accounting qualification.

A guide to the assessment

chapter 1

The accounting function

- Introduction.
- The accounting function.
- Relationships with other departments.
- Coordination between accounting and other business functions.
- Regulations affecting the accounting function.
- Understanding systems.

The accounting function

Introduction

Organisations and the need for control

Definition
'Organisations are social arrangements for the controlled performance of collective goals'.

Control mechanisms

Methods of control
Organisational structure
Target setting and budgeting
Direct supervision
Culture
Self-control
Control Systems – e.g. actual v budget
Control processes – e.g. control account reconciliations

Organisational Structure

How to discuss structure
The division of responsibility
The degree of decentralisation
The length of the scalar chain
The size of the span of control
Whether organisations are 'tall' or 'flat'

The accounting function

The role of the accounting function

There are four components to the function

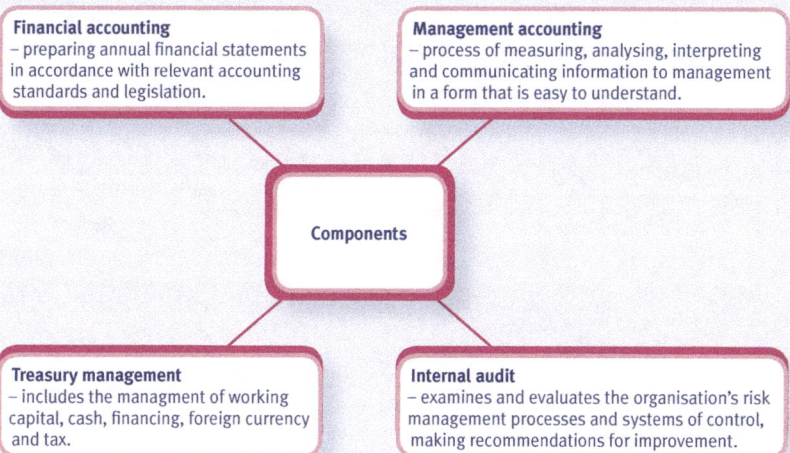

The accounting function

Relationships with other departments

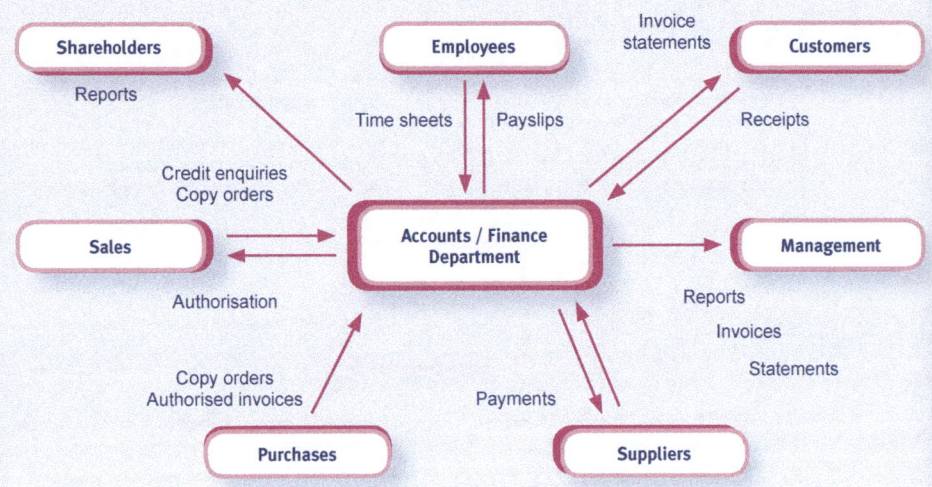

Coordination between accounting and other business functions

Department	Areas of interaction
Purchasing	Establishing credit terms Monitoring payments Inventory and cost control
Production	Cost measurements and overhead allocation Budgeting (e.g. units, quantity) Achieving efficiency and economy
HR	Recruitment and training expenditure Salary payment, estimating PAYE liabilities Reward plans, tax-efficient benefits packages
IT	Systems design and development Improving access to information Incorporating new technology into operations
Customer services	Pricing additional services (e.g. maintenance) Assessing costs of product failures Qualitative feedback on operations
Marketing	Advertising budgets Product pricing Estimating market share

Regulations affecting the accounting function

Responsibility to regulatory authorities:

- Companies House (e.g. submission of financial statement for inspection by interested parties).
- Tax authorities (e.g. HMRC for VAT, PAYE, corporation tax).
- Financial services (e.g. stock exchange for listed companies).
- Regulators, where appropriate (e.g. Charities Commission, Ofcom).

Companies Act 1985 sets out that financial statements have to give a "true and fair view".

IFRS Foundation supervises the development of international standards and guidance. It's a parent entity of:

- International Accounting Standards Board (IASB): aims to develop a single set of quality, understandable and enforceable accounting standards.
- FRS Interpretation Committee (IFRS IC): reviews widespread accounting issues and provides guidance.
- IFRS Advisory Council (IFRS AC): consults the users of financial information and offers advice to the IFRS Foundation.

Understanding systems

General systems

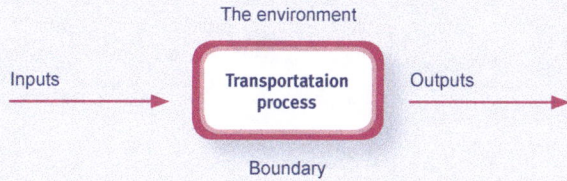

Example – If we are concentrating on the finance system, then sales, production and purchasing become part of the environment, and within the system boundary will be found smaller subsystems such as product costing, financial accounting and treasury.

Control systems

- **Standard** – is what the system is aiming for.
- **Sensor** (or detector) – measures the output of the system.
- **Comparator** – compares the information from the standard and the sensor.
- **Effector** (or activator) – initiates the control action.
- **Feedback** – is the information that is taken from the system output and used to adjust the system.

The accounting function

chapter 2

The use of key financial reports

- Financial accounting and financial statements.
- Management accounting and management reports.
- User groups.

Financial accounting and financial statements

Purpose of financial statements

The statement of financial position	Provides information on the financial position of a business (its assets and liabilities at a point in time).
The statement of profit or loss	Provides information on the performance of a business (the profit or loss which results from trading over a period of time).
The statement of other comprehensive income	Shows income and expenses that are not recognised in profit or loss.
The statement of changes in equity	Provides information about how the equity of the company has changed over the period.
The statement of cash flow	Provides information on the financial adaptability of a business (the movement of cash into and out of the business over a period of time).

Stewardship

Stewardship is the accountability of management for the resources entrusted to it by the owners or the Government.

Management accounting and management reports

Needs of management

Planning	Planning involves establishing the objectives of an organisation and formulating relevant strategies that can be used to achieve those objectives.
Decision making	In most situations, decision making involves making a choice between two or more alternatives.
Control	Output from operations is measured and reported ('fed back') to management, and actual results are compared against the plan in control reports.
	Managers take corrective action where appropriate, especially in the case of exceptionally bad or good performance.

Key reports

- Budget reports, detailing budgetary plans for future periods
- Variance reports comparing actual and budget performance, to facilitate effective control
- Reports of key performance indicators to ensure that management focus on what is important to the success of the organisation.
- One-off reports that look at individual decisions.

Evaluating a management report – factors to consider

- The basis of preparation
- The methods used
- The figures used
- The impact on people concerned

User groups

Needs of users

Investors	Need to be able to assess the ability of a business to pay dividends and manage resources.
Management	Need information with which to assess performance, take decisions, plan, and control the business.
Employees and their unions	Need information to help them negotiate pay and benefits.
Customers	Need to be assured that their supply will continue into the future.
Suppliers	Need to be assured that they will continue to get paid and on time and the financial statements will help with this.
Lenders, such as banks	Interested in the ability of the business to pay interest and repay loans.
HM Revenue and Customs	Uses financial statements as the basis for tax assessments.
The public (especially pressure groups)	Will look at the financial reports and statements to aid their understanding of profits an organisation may be making from activities to which the pressure group are opposed.

chapter 3

Internal controls

- Internal control.
- Typical control activities (SPAM SOAP).
- Internal audit.
- The purchases cycle.
- The sales Sales cycle.
- Payroll.
- Cash and cheques.
- Segregation of duties revisited.

Internal control

Internal control consists of the following components (ISA 315):

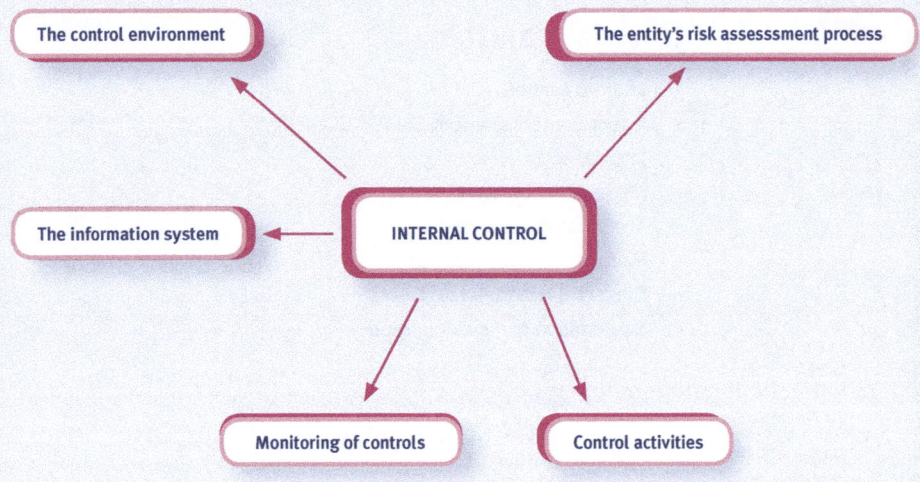

Typical control activities (SPAM SOAP)

Segregation of duties	Keep separate the custodial function, the authorisation function, the recording function and the execution function.
Physical controls	Access to assets and records is only permitted to authorised personnel.
Authorisation and approval	All transactions require authorisation or approval by a responsible person.
Management	Controls exercised by the management outside the day-to-day routine of the system.
Supervision	Supervisory procedures by the management.
Organisation	A well-defined organisational structure showing how responsibility and authority are delegated.
Arithmetical and accounting	E.g. control accounts, cross totals, reconciliations and sequential controls over documents.
Personnel	Well-motivated, competent personnel who possess the necessary integrity for their tasks.

Internal audit

Definition

'an independent, objective assurance and consulting activity designed to add value and improve an organisation's operations.'

What do internal auditors do?

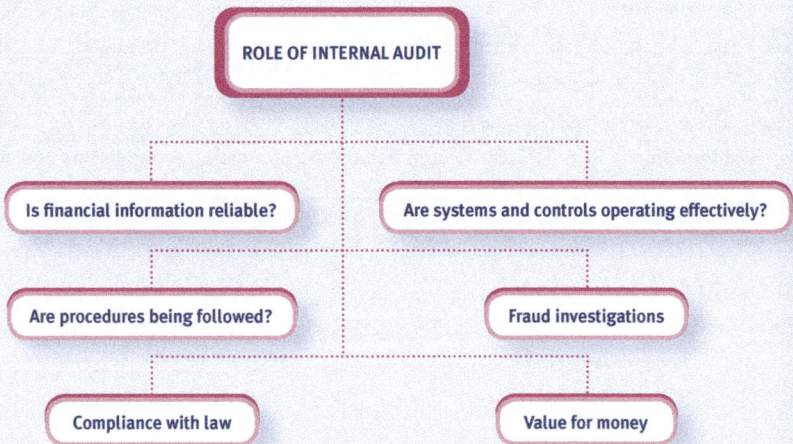

The purchases cycle

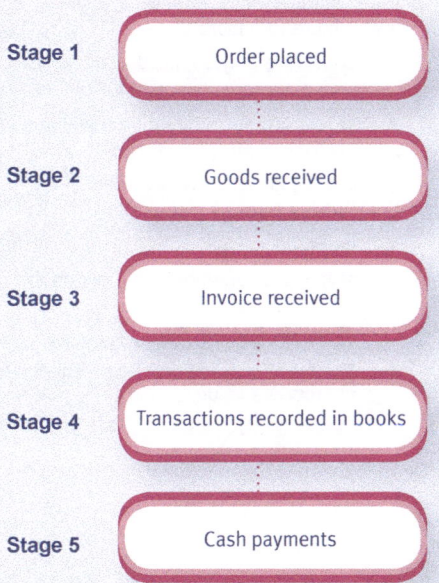

Purchase system

The objectives of controls in the purchase system are to ensure that:

- all purchases are of the appropriate quality and price
- only necessary goods/services are procured
- all purchases and related payables are recorded
- expenditure is recorded in the period to which it relates
- expenditure is recorded accurately and related payables are recorded at an appropriate value.

Internal controls

The sales cycle

- **Stage 1**: Order received
- **Stage 2**: Goods despatched
- **Stage 3**: Invoice sent
- **Stage 4**: Transactions recorded in books
- **Stage 5**: Cash received

Sales system

The objectives of controls in the sales system are to ensure that:

- goods are only supplied to customers who pay promptly and in full
- orders are despatched promptly and in full to the correct customer
- only valid sales are recorded
- all sales and related receivables are recorded
- revenue is recorded in the period to which it relates
- sales are recorded accurately and related receivables are recorded at an appropriate value.

Payroll

- **Stage 1**: Clock cards submitted and input
- **Stage 2**: Gross pay, deductions and net pay calculated
- **Stage 3**: Other amendements input
- **Stage 4**: Final payroll calculated and payslips produced
- **Stage 5**: Payments to employees and tax authorities
- **Stage 6**: Payroll costs and payments recorded

Payroll system

The objectives of controls in the payroll system are to ensure that:

- only genuine employees are paid
- employees are only paid for work done
- employees are paid at the correct rates of pay
- gross pay is calculated and recorded accurately
- net pay is calculated and recorded accurately; and
- correct amounts owed are recorded and paid to the taxation authorities.

Internal controls

Cash and cheques

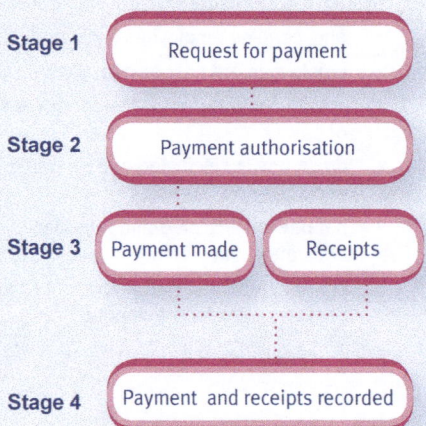

Cash cycle

The objectives of controls in the cash cycle are to ensure that:

- petty cash levels are kept to a minimum, preventing theft
- payments can only be made for legitimate business expenditure
- cash and chequebooks are safeguarded
- receipts are banked on a timely basis
- cash movements are recorded on a timely basis.

Segregation of duties revisited

Purchases	The persons who raise purchase orders should be independent of the ledger keeping function, the stock recording and control subsystem and the cheque.
Sales	The persons responsible for preparation of sales orders should be independent of credit control, custody of stock and recording sales transactions.
	The credit controller should be independent of the sales order clerks.
	The warehouse/despatch department should be independent of sales order preparation, credit control and invoicing.
	Sales invoicing should be independent of sales order preparation, credit control, warehouse and despatch departments.
	The sales ledger clerk should be independent of sales order preparation, credit control, warehouse, despatch and sales invoicing.
	The sales ledger control account should be maintained independent of the sales ledger clerk.
Cash	The persons who sign the cheques should be different from those who handle the authorisation of purchase invoices.
	The persons who are responsible for opening the post, preparing the paying-in details and controlling the sales ledger should be separate functionaries.

Internal controls

chapter 4

Internal controls in computerised systems

- Information systems controls.
- Data security.
- Integrity controls.
- Controls.
- Systems integrity in a network environment.
- Contingency controls.

Information systems controls

General controls

General controls relate to the environment within which computer-based systems are developed, maintained and operated and are generally applicable to all the applications running on the system.

Personnel recruitment policies	To ensure honesty and competence.
Segregation of duties	To minimise tampering with programs or data.
Proper **training** programmes	To ensure competence and reduce errors.
Physical security of hardware and software	To prevent accidental or malicious damage or natural disasters.
Authorisation procedures for program amendments and testing	To prevent unwanted changes being made.
Back-up procedures (maintaining copies of files off-site, back-up facilities).	To ensure data and systems can be recovered.
Access controls.	e.g. firewalls and anti-virus checkers.
Hacking prevention measures	To ensure the system is not accessed during data transmission (hacking).
Efficiency measures	Controls to ensure that the computing resources are used efficiently.

Data Security

Data security measures involve different aspects:

- **Physical security**, such as the security of data storage facilities, from flood as well as unauthorised access
- **Software security**, such as maintaining a log of all failed access requests, and
- **Operational security**, with regard to such things as work data being taken home by employees, and periodic data protection audits of the computer systems.

Physical Security controls

Fire systems and procedures	e.g. fire alarms, heat and smoke detectors.
Location of hardware	e.g. away from risk of flooding.
Regular building maintenance	e.g. attention to roofs, windows and doors will reduce the risk of water penetration and make forcible entry more difficult.
Physical access controls	e.g. security guards to check identification and authorisation, CCTV, using badge readers or coded locks on access doors from public areas and electronic tagging of hardware.

Internal controls in computerised systems

Individual staff controls

Logical access system	e.g. identification of the user, authentication of user identity and checks on user authority.
Personal identification	e.g. PIN, fingerprint recognition, eye retina 'prints' and voice 'prints'.
Storage of CDs, removable data storage devices in secure locations	e.g. back-up data is stored in a fire-proof environment on-site, and occasionally some form of master back-up is removed from the installation site completely.

Integrity controls

Activities

Data integrity means completeness and accuracy of data. For decisions to be made consistently throughout the organisation, it is necessary for the system to contain controls over the input, processing and output of data to maintain its integrity.

Input activities	File processing activities	Output activities
- data collection and preparation - data authorisation - data conversion (if appropriate) - data transmission - data correction - corrected data re-input	- data validation and edit - data manipulation, sorting/merging - master file updating	- output control and reconciliation with predetermined data - information distribution

Internal controls in computerised systems

Controls

Input Controls	Validation and processing controls	Output controls
• Verification • Type checks • Non-existence checks • Consistency checks • Duplication checks • Range checks • Input comparisons • Batch and hash totals • One-for-one checks	**Validation** • Comparison of totals • Comparison of data sets • Sequence numbers • Range checks • Format checks **Processing** • Standardisation • Batch control • Double processing	• Batch control totals • Start or report / page number / end of report markers • Distribution lists

Systems integrity in a network environment

Risks

- Hardware/software disruption or malfunction
- Computer viruses
- Unauthorised access to the system

Controls

- Physical access controls
- User identification
- Data and program access authorisation
- Program integrity controls
- Database integrity controls
- Anti-virus software
- Surveillance
- Communication lines safeguards
- Encryption
- Firewalls

Contingency controls

Disasters

In computing terms, a disaster might mean the loss or unavailability of some of the computer systems.

Contingency Plan

- Standby procedures – so that essential operations can be performed while normal services are disrupted.
- Recovery procedures – to return to normal working once the breakdown is fixed.
- Management policies – to ensure that the plan is implemented.

- **Controls**
- Distributed support, where computing is spread over several sites.
- Reciprocal agreement with another company.
- A commercial computer bureau.
- Empty rooms / equipped rooms.
- Relocatable computer centres.

chapter 5

Ratio analysis

- Ratio calculations.
- Interpreting ratios.
- Interpreting financial information.
- Limitations of ratio analysis.
- Linking ratios and control problems.

Ratio analysis

Ratio calculations

Profitability
- ROCE
- Gross profit
- Operating profit
- Asset turnover

Liquidity
- Current ratio
- Quick ratio
- Inventories days
- Receivables days
- Payables days

Gearing
- Gearing
- Interest cover

Investor
- EPS
- Dividend yield
- Dividend cover
- P/E ratio

Profitability

$$ROCE = \frac{PBIT}{Capital\ Employed\ (Equity + Debt)} \times 100\%$$

$$Gross\ profit\ margin = \frac{Gross\ profit}{Revenue} \times 100\%$$

$$Operating\ profit\ margin = \frac{PBIT}{Revenue} \times 100\%$$

$$Asset\ turnover = \frac{Revenue}{Capital\ Employed} \times 100\%$$

Short-term liquidity

$$\text{Current ratio} = \frac{\text{Current Assets}}{\text{Current liabilities}} :1$$

$$\text{Quick ratio} = \frac{\text{Current Assets} - \text{Inventory}}{\text{Current liabilities}}$$

Efficiency ratios (working capital)

$$\text{Inventory days} = \frac{\text{Inventories}}{\text{COS}} \times 365 \text{ days}$$

$$\text{Trade receivables collection period} = \frac{\text{Trade receivables}}{\text{Revenue}} \times 365 \text{ days}$$

$$\text{Trade payables collection period} = \frac{\text{Trade payables}}{\text{Purchases (or COS)}} \times 365 \text{ days}$$

Long-term solvency

$$\text{Gearing} = \frac{\text{Debt}}{\text{Equity}} \times 100\% \text{ or } \frac{\text{Debt}}{\text{Debt} + \text{Equity}}$$

$$\text{Interest cover} = \frac{\text{Profit before interest and tax}}{\text{Interest}}$$

Investor ratios

$$\text{EPS} = \frac{\text{Earnings}}{\text{Shares}}$$

$$\text{Dividend yield} = \frac{\text{Dividend per share}}{\text{MV per share}} \times 100\%$$

$$\text{Dividend cover} = \frac{\text{PAT}}{\text{Dividend}}$$

$$\text{P/E ratio} = \frac{\text{Price per share}}{\text{Earnings per share}}$$

Interpreting ratios

Exam focus

It is important to understand the meaning of the ratios as well as calculating them for the exam.

Interpreting financial information

Introduction

Financial statements on their own are of limited use. In this chapter we will consider how to interpret them and gain additional useful information from them.

Users of financial statements

When interpreting financial statements it is important to ascertain who are the users of accounts and what information they need:

- shareholders and potential investors – primarily concerned with receiving an adequate return on their investment, but it must at least provide security and liquidity
- suppliers and lenders – concerned with the security of their debt or loan
- management – concerned with the trend and level of profits, since this is the main measure of their success.

Commenting on ratios

Ratios are of limited use on their own, thus, the following points should serve as a useful checklist if you need to analyse the data and comment on it:

- What does the ratio literally mean?
- What does a change in the ratio mean?
- What is the norm?
- What are the limitations of the ratio?

Limitations of ratio analysis

- Ratios do not provide answers; they merely highlight significant features or trends in the financial statements. They usually highlight areas that need further investigation.
- Be mindful of seasonal trade as accounting year-ends are often just after the seasonal trend is over when the business is at its best.
- Watch out for window dressing in the financial statements such as collecting receivables just before the year-end in order to show a larger cash balance and lower receivables than is normal.
- Accounting ratios are based on accounting information and are only as accurate as that underlying accounting information.
- If comparisons are to be made they must be with companies with a similar trade, otherwise the pattern of ratios will be different and the comparisons meaningless.

Linking ratios and control problems

From problems to ratios – examples

Control issue	Impact on financial statements	Key ratios affected
Fraud where items are stolen from the warehouse	• Cost of sales will higher than expected	• Fall in gross and net margins
Credit controller ill	• Receivables balance will be higher than expected	• Receivables days higher • Quick and current ratios higher
Theft of cash	• Less cash than expected	• Quick and current ratios lower
Fraud where items are sold to a friend at a very low price	• Sales lower than expected • Gross profit lower than expected	• Fall in gross and net margins • Receivables days lower

From ratios to problems – examples

Ratio	Basic causes	Possible control issues
Gross margin down	• Prices lower and / or costs of sales higher	• Sales managers giving excessive discounts • Theft of inventory • Excessive waste / obsolescence of stock • Cut-off problems • Price rises from suppliers unchecked due to purchase orders not being authorised correctly
Inventory days higher	• Excessive period – end inventory • Cost of sales lower	• Purchased too much inventory due to purchase orders not being checked properly • Purchase invoices mis-recorded • Errors with time sheets

Ratio analysis

chapter 6

Fraud

- What is fraud?
- Fraud risk management.
- Fraud detection.
- Fraud response.

Fraud

What is fraud?

Definitions

- Dishonestly obtaining an advantage, avoiding an obligation or causing a loss to another party.
- Note: distinction made between fraud and errors (unintentional mistakes).

Examples of fraud

Crimes against customers	e.g. pyramid schemes; selling counterfeit goods
Employee fraud against employers	e.g. falsifying expense claims
Crimes against investors, consumers and employees	e.g. falsifying financial statements
Crimes against financial institutions	e.g. fraudulent insurance claims
Crimes against government	e.g. social security benefit claims fraud; tax evasion
Crimes by professional criminals	e.g. money laundering
E-crime by people using computers	e.g. spamming; copyright crimes; hacking

Fraud risk management

Prerequisites for fraud

- An ability to rationalise the fraudulent action and hence act with dishonesty.
- A perceived opportunity to commit fraud.
- A motive, incentive or pressure to commit fraud.

Fraud prevention

- Anti-fraud culture
- Risk awareness
- Whistleblowing
- Sound internal control systems

Fraud deterrence

Only when potential fraudsters believe fraud will be detected and when whistle-blowers believe they will be protected will there be an effective deterrence of fraud.

Fraud detection

- Performing regular checks.
- Warning signals/fraud risk indicators.
- Failures in internal control procedures
    - Lack of information provided to auditors
    - Unusual behaviour by individual staff members
    - Accounting difficulties.
- Whistleblowers.

Fraud response

- Response plan:
    - Internal disciplinary action
    - Civil litigation
    - Criminal prosecution
    - Responsibilities clearly set out

Fraud

chapter 7

Improving the accounting system

- Reasons for change.
- Justification of change.
- Implementing changes – dealing with resistance.
- Implementing changes – approaches.

Reasons for change

Reason for change	Example
Regulation changes	VAT rules change
Growth	Old manual approach cannot cope with growth
New information flow	The government could introduce new report requirements
Short-term capacity issues	PC failure
Identified weakness	e.g. need to introduce new levels of authorisation
Changes in the environment	Increased focus on environmental factors
New products	Switch to ABC

Justification of change

Cost-benefit analysis

Tangible costs	Intangible costs
- One-off costs (e.g. development, buying new equipment) - On-going costs (e.g. maintenance, replaceable items)	- Staff dissatisfaction if systems are poorly specified or implemented. - The cost of increased staff mistakes and reduced performance during the learning period after a new system is implemented. - Opportunity costs. - Lock-in costs. Purchasing a particular solution can bind a company to a particular supplier, reducing its ability to take advantage of future developments from other providers.
Tangible benefits	**Intangible benefits**
- Savings in staff salaries, maintenance costs and consumables. - Greater efficiency. - Business benefits gained through improved management information. - Gaining competitive advantage.	- More informed or quicker decision-making. - Improved customer service, resulting in increased customer satisfaction. - Freedom from routine decisions and activities, resulting in more time being available for strategic planning and innovation. - Better understanding of customer needs through improved analysis of data.

Techniques

- Payback
- NPV
- SWOT

Implementing changes – dealing with resistance

Resistance

Job Factors	These generally revolve around fear – fear of new technology, fear of change or fear of demotion or levels of pay.
Social Factors	The people affected may dislike the potential new social dynamic (or like the existing social scene and not want that to change).
Personal factors	These, by definition, are more varied as each person may react differently to a particular change.

Response

Source of resistance	Possible response
• The need for security and the familiar.	• Provide information and encouragement, invite involvement.
• Having the opinion that no change is needed.	• Clarify the purpose of the change and how it will be made.
• Trying to protect vested interests.	• Demonstrate the problem or the opportunity that makes changes desirable.
• Dislike the social upheaval.	• Organise social team building events.

Implementing changes – approaches

Testing

Realistic data testing	The new system is tested against normal transactions to ensure it operates as expected.
Contrived testing	The new system is presented with unusual data to see how it reacts e.g. negative sales invoices.
Volume testing	A common problem with systems is that they fail to cope when volumes increase, so this is tested in advance. Systems may crash or slow down excessively.
User acceptance testing	Systems are often designed by IT experts but then used by people with much less IT skill.

Changeover method

Direct	The old system ceases and the new system takes over on the same day.
Parallel	In this system both the old and new systems are run at the same time.
Pilot	The new system is piloted in a particular location. In this way operational bugs can be identified and removed before wider implementation takes place.
Phased	This is similar to a pilot, but it is the phrase used when the system is introduced in stages or in one sub system at a time.

Improving the accounting system

chapter 8

Ethics and sustainability

- Ethics.
- Fundamental principles.
- Examples.
- Sustainability.
- Benefits of acting sustainably.
- Sustainability and the accounting system.

Ethics

What is ethics?

- Morality – the difference between right and wrong – 'doing the right thing'.
- How one should act in a certain situation.

Why should we bother with ethics?

Pros	Cons
- To protect the public interest - To avoid discipline/fines - Improved reputation - Good ethics can attract customers - Good ethics can result in a more effective workforce - Ethics can give cost savings - Ethics can reduce risk	- Increased cost of sourcing materials from ethical sources - Lose profit by not trading with unethical customers/suppliers - Waste of management time?

Fundamental principles

Confidentiality	Information obtained in a business relationship is not to be disclosed to third parties without specific authority being given to do so, unless there is a legal or professional reason to do so.
Objectivity	Business or professional judgement is not compromised because of bias or conflict of interest.
Integrity	This implies fair dealing and truthfulness.
Professional Competence and Due Care	The necessary professional knowledge and skills required to carry out work should be present.
Professional Behaviour	All relevant laws and regulations must be complied with and any actions that would bring the profession into disrepute avoided.

Ethics and sustainability

Examples

Accounting issues	Creative accounting.
	Directors' pay.
	Bribes.
	Insider trading.
Production	Should the company produce certain products at all, e.g. tobacco.
	Should the company be concerned about the effects on the environment of its production processes?
	Should the company test its products on animals?
Sales / marketing	Price fixing and anticompetitive behaviour.
	Is it ethical to target advertising at children?
	Should products be advertised by junk mail or spam email?
Personnel	Discrimination.
	The contract of employment must offer a fair balance of power between employee and employer.
	The workplace must be a safe and healthy place to operate in.

Sustainability

What do we mean by 'sustainability'?

- Sustainable development is development that meets the needs of the **present** without compromising the ability of **future** generations to meet their own needs.

    (The UN's Bruntland Report).

- A sustainable business is a business that offers products and services that fulfil society's needs while placing an equal emphasis on **people**, **planet** and **profits**.

    (The Sustainable Business Network)

Examples of unsustainable practices

Economic

- Underpayment of taxes – not contributing to maintaining the country's infrastructure (schools, roads, etc.).
- Bribery and corruption.

Social

- Rich companies exploiting third world labour as cheap manufacturing.

Environmental

- Long term damage to the environment from carbon dioxide and other greenhouse gases.

Benefits of acting sustainably

- Potential cost savings – e.g. due to lower energy usage.
- Avoiding fines – e.g. for pollution.
- Short term gain in sales – e.g. if customers are influenced by sustainability related labels on products.
- Long term gain in sales – e.g. due to enhanced PR and reputation.
- Better risk management – e.g. pre-empting changes in regulations.
- Sustainability is one aspects of a firm's commitment to CSR.

Sustainability and the accounting system

The Accountancy Department

- The paperless office – how much of the paper used in the accounting department is justified?
- Emailing invoices to customers rather than posting paper versions.
- Emailing statements to customers rather than posting paper versions.
- The energy usage for lights, the machines and for heating.
- The use of sustainable materials for the office furniture.
- The level of carbon dioxide produced (if any).

'What gets measured gets done'

- The accountancy function can help champion sustainability by suggesting environmental performance measures and measuring these KPIs.

Ethics and sustainability

chapter 9

Recap of key aspects of Financial Statements of Limited Companies

- IFRS foundation.
- Legal framework.
- IASB framework.
- IAS 1 Presentation of Financial Statements.
- The fundamental principles of the AAT Code of Professional Ethics.
- The threats.
- Safeguards.
- Uses of ratios.
- Key ratios.
- Limitations of ratio analysis.

Recap of key aspects of Financial Statements of Limited Companies

IFRS foundation

The structure of the International Financial Reporting Standards Foundation (IFRS Foundation) and its subsidiary bodies is shown below:

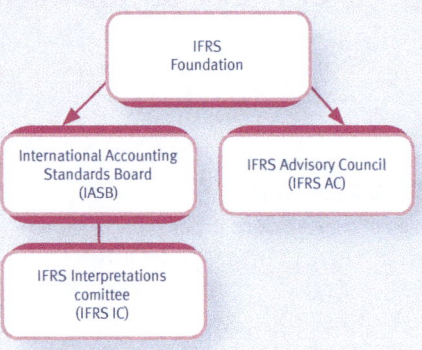

Key Point

- The IFRS Foundation is an independent not for profit foundation based in the US whose trustees appoint the members of the IASB, IFRS AC and IFRS IC.

- The IASB is responsible for developing and issuing new accounting standards. The IASB issues International Financial Reporting Standards (IFRSs) and has adopted the previous International Accounting Standards (IASs).

- The IFRS AC advises the IASB on priorities in its work and informs the IASB of the implications of proposed standards for users and preparers of financial statements.

- The IFRS IC draws up interpretations if a new problem arises or gives guidance on the application of a standard where unsatisfactory interpretations exist.

Legal framework

- In the UK, companies must prepare their financial statements following the rules laid out in the Companies Act 2006 (CA06).
- The CA06 has been amended to reflect the fact that some companies prepare their financial statements based upon the application of IFRSs.
- In the UK, the Financial Reporting Council (FRC) prepares accounting standards. In recent years there has been a process of harmonisation between UK and International standards and the majority of UK standards are now equivalent to IFRSs.

IASB framework

The IASB's Conceptual Framework for Financial Reporting identifies the principles on which accounting standards are to be developed. It aims to assist in the preparation of financial statements, development of new standards and to reduce alternative accounting treatments.

Key Point

- The underlying assumption of financial statements is that they are prepared on a going concern basis.
- There are two fundamental qualitative characteristics together with four enhancing characteristics:

The two fundamental qualitative characteristics:

- **Relevance** – financial information is regarded as relevant if it capable of influencing the decision of users.
- **Faithful representation** – this means that financial information must be complete, neutral and free from error.

The four enhancing qualititative characteristics:

- **Comparability** – it should be possible to compare an entity over time and with similar information about other entities.
- **Verifiability** – if information can be verified (e.g. through an audit) this provides assurance to the users that it is both credible and reliable.
- **Timeliness** – information should be provided to users within a timescale suitable for their decision making purposes.
- **Understandability** – information should be understandable to those that might want to review and use it. This can be facilitated through appropriate classification, characterisation and presentation of information.

Elements of the financial statements

Asset: a resource controlled by an entity as a result of past events and from which future economic benefits are expected to flow to the entity.

Liability: a present obligation of the entity arising from past events, the settlement of which is expected to result in an outflow from the enterprise of resources embodying economic benefits.

Equity: the residual interest in the assets of the entity after deducting all its liabilities.

Income: income consists of both revenue and gains. Revenue arises from a business's ordinary activities such as the sale of goods. Gains represent increases in economic benefits such as a gain on disposal of a non-current asset and are not normally shown within revenue.

Expenses: expenses are losses as well as expenses that arise in the normal course of business such as cost of sales, wages and depreciation. Losses represent a decrease in economic benefits such as losses on disposal of non-current assets or disasters such as fire or flood and are often shown separately in the financial statements.

Recognition of items in the financial statements

Recognition of (i.e. recording) an item in the financial statements occurs if:

- the item meets the definition of an element
- it is probable that any future economic benefit associated with the item will flow to or from the entity
- it can be measured at a monetary amount with sufficient reliability.

IAS 1 Presentation of Financial Statements

IAS 1 provides formats for the statement of profit or loss, statement of financial position and statement of changes in equity as well as setting out six accounting concepts that should be applied:

- **going concern** – the business will continue in operation for the foreseeable future
- **accruals** – the effects of transactions and other events are recognised as they occur and not as cash or its equivalent is received or paid
- **consistency of presentation** – items in the financial statements are presented and classified in the same way from one period to the next unless there is a change in the operations of the business or a new standard requires a change in presentation
- **materiality and aggregation** – each material class of similar items shall be presented separately in the financial statements
- **offsetting** – assets and liabilities and income and expenses cannot be offset unless a standard requires it
- **comparative information** – should be shown for all amounts reported in the financial statements.

Accounting policies should be selected so that the financial statements comply with all international standards and interpretations.

An entity must make an explicit statement in the notes to the financial statements that they comply with IFRS.

The fundamental principles of the AAT Code of Professional Ethics

Outlined below are the key principles of the AAT Code of Professional Ethics.

Professional competence and due care

A professional accountant has a continuing duty to maintain professional knowledge and skill at the level required to ensure that a client or employer receives competent professional service based on current developments in practice, legislation and techniques.

Objectivity

A professional accountant should not allow bias, conflict of interest or undue influence of others to override professional or business judgements.

Confidentiality

A professional accountant should respect the confidentiality of information acquired as a result of professional and business relationships and should not disclose any such information to third parties without proper and specific authority unless there is a legal or professional right or duty to disclose.

Professional behaviour

A person should not act in any way that is unprofessional or does not comply with relevant laws and regulations.

Integrity

A person should be straightforward and honest in performing professional work and in all business relationships.

The threats

The following are all examples of behaviour that could threaten an accountant's objectivity or independence from their clients:

The self-interest threat – may occur because of a financial or other interest held by the accountant or a family member.

The advocacy threat – may occur when an accountant is asked to promote or represent their client in some way. In this situation the accountant would have to be biased in favour of the client and therefore cannot be objective.

The self-review threat – when work you have previously prepared needs review – you cannot audit your own work.

The familiarity or trust threat – this occurs when the accountant is too sympathetic or trusting of the client because of a close relationship with them.

The intimidation threat – may occur when an accountant may be deterred from acting objectively by threats – actual or perceived.

Safeguards

Safeguards are controls to reduce or eliminate threats. They fall into two broad categories:

(i) Safeguards created by the profession, legislation or regulation. Examples of these include:

- Educational, training and experience requirements for entry into the profession.
- Continuing professional development requirements.
- Corporate governance regulations.
- Professional standards.

- External review by a legally empowered third party of the reports, returns, communications or information produced by a professional accountant.

(ii) Safeguards in the work environment. Examples of these include:

- Policies and procedures to implement and monitor quality control of engagements.
- A disciplinary procedure to promote compliance with policies and procedures.
- Policies and procedures to monitor and, if necessary, manage the reliance on revenue received from a single client.

Recap of key aspects of Financial Statements of Limited Companies

Uses of ratios

Key Point

- Ratio analysis is a means of interpreting financial statements.
- Users will review the financial statements and make decisions based on the information given. Ratios are calculated and compared with:
  - the performance of the business in previous years
  - the budgeted or planned performance in the current year
  - the performance of similar businesses.
- Ratios can assist in pointing the user of the financial statements to areas where the company may be performing particularly well or badly. They do not in themselves provide an answer but they can help in indicating the right direction for further investigation.
- The types of ratio to use will depend on the user of the information. For example, banks and lenders will be interested in liquidity ratios; management will be interested in profitability ratios.
- Ratios fall into several categories:
  - profitability ratios
  - liquidity and working capital ratios
  - investor ratios.

Key ratios

CBA focus

Ratios are important tools to assist in the interpretation of financial statements. You must learn these ratios and be able to calculate and interpret them as an exam task will require you to do both.

Profitability ratios

- **Return on capital employed (ROCE) =**

  $$\frac{\text{Profit from operations}}{\text{Total equity + Non-current liabilities}} \times 100$$

  ROCE is very important as it shows the profit generated from the capital employed in the business. If ROCE has increased it is due to either increases in profitability and/or increases in asset utilisation.

- **Return on shareholder's funds =**

  $$\frac{\text{Profit after tax}}{\text{Total equity}} \times 100$$

- **Gross profit percentage =**

  $$\frac{\text{Gross profit}}{\text{Revenue}} \times 100$$

  This shows the profit made on revenue before accounting for overhead costs. An increase or decrease may be due to a change in the sales mix, changes in costs or selling prices.

Recap of key aspects of Financial Statements of Limited Companies

- **Expense/Revenue percentage**

  $$\frac{\text{Specified expense}}{\text{Revenue}} \times 100$$

- This can apply to any expense

- **Operating profit percentage =**

  $$\frac{\text{Profit from operations}}{\text{Revenue}} \times 100$$

  This shows the profitability after taking into account expenses. A change may be due to changes in costs. You might expect an increase if sales have increased, but must watch out for costs that are rising above any sales increase as it may be that costs are not being controlled.

Liquidity

- **The current ratio =**

  $$\frac{\text{Current assets}}{\text{Current liabilities}}$$

- **The quick ratio =**

  $$\frac{\text{Current assets} - \text{inventory}}{\text{Current liabilities}}$$

These two ratios show whether a business can cover its current liabilities from current assets. The quick ratio removes inventory as this is the least liquid current asset. If the ratio is too low, it may suggest the business will have trouble paying current liabilities and if the ratio is too high it may suggest that working capital is not being used efficiently.

This ratio can vary greatly from industry to industry.

Use of resources

- **Inventory turnover =**
  $$\frac{\text{Cost of sales}}{\text{Inventories}}$$

- Companies have to strike a balance between being able to satisfy customers' requirements from inventory and the cost of having too much capital tied up in inventory.

- **Inventory holding period =**
  $$\frac{\text{Inventories}}{\text{Cost of sales}} \times 365 \text{ days}$$

  This shows how long inventory is being held before use.

- **Asset turnover (net assets) =**
  $$\frac{\text{Revenue}}{\text{Total assets - current liabilities}}$$

- **Trade receivables collection period =**
  $$\frac{\text{Trade receivables}}{\text{Revenue}} \times 365 \text{ days}$$

  If the receivables collection period becomes too high, the business may suffer from poor cash flow. Retail companies do not usually have receivables so this ratio would be irrelevant for those companies.

- **Trade payables payment period =**
  $$\frac{\text{Trade payables}}{\text{Cost of sales}} \times 365 \text{ days}$$

  Extending the payables payment period can be a cheap source of finance but companies run the risk of upsetting suppliers and not being offered credit in the future.

- **Working Capital Cycle =**
  Inventory days + Receivables days – Payables days.

- **Asset turnover (non-current assets) =**
  $$\frac{\text{Revenue}}{\text{non-current assets}}$$

Recap of key aspects of Financial Statements of Limited Companies

Financial position

- **Interest cover =**

  $$\frac{\text{Profit from operations}}{\text{Finance costs}}$$

- This shows how many times the interest charge can be paid out of the current profits. It is a measure of security - the higher the ratio, the more secure the interest payment.

- **Gearing =**

  $$\frac{\text{Non-current liabilities}}{\text{Total equity + Non-current liabilities}}$$

- This ratio shows the proportion of debt to total finance in the business (equity plus debt). The higher the gearing ratio, the riskier a company is seen to be as debt interest must be paid out before dividends.

Limitations of ratio analysis

- Ratios do not provide answers; they merely highlight significant features or trends in the financial statements. They usually highlight areas that need further investigation.
- Be mindful of seasonal trade as accounting year-ends are often just after the seasonal trend is over when the business is at its best.
- Watch out for window dressing in the financial statements such as collecting receivables just before the year-end in order to show a larger cash balance and lower receivables than is normal.
- Accounting ratios are based on accounting information and are only as accurate as that underlying accounting information.
- If comparisons are to be made they must be with companies with a similar trade, otherwise the pattern of ratios will be different and the comparisons meaningless.

chapter 10

Recap of key aspects of Management Accounting: Budgeting

- Behavioural aspects of budgeting.
- Basic methods of budgeting.
- Flexed budgets.
- Flexible budgets.
- Materials variances.
- Labour variances.
- Interdependence of variances.
- Variance investigation.
- Reasons for variances.
- Performance indicators.

Behavioural aspects of budgeting

Target setting and motivation

Targets will assist motivation and appraisal if they are at the right level.

- Too hard and people give up.
- Too easy and people won't try hard enough.

An ideal target should be slightly above the anticipated performance level.

Targets should be:

- Communicated in advance.
- Dependent on factors controllable by the individual.
- Based on quantifiable factors.
- Linked to appropriate rewards and penalties.
- Chosen carefully to ensure goal congruence.
- Challenging but achievable.

Participation is generally agreed to help.

Participation

Top-down budgeting (non-participative)

A budget which is set without allowing the ultimate budget holder to have the opportunity to participate in the budgeting process.

Bottom-up budgeting (participative)

A system of budgeting in which budget holders have the opportunity to participate in setting their own budgets.

Advantages of participative budgets	Disadvantages of participative budgets
1. Increased motivation.	1. Senior managers may resent loss of control.
2. Should contain better information, especially in a fast-moving or diverse business.	2. Bad decisions from inexperienced managers.
3. Increases managers' understanding and commitment.	3. Budgets may not be in line with corporate objectives.
4. Better communication.	4. Budget preparation is slower and disputes can arise.
5. Senior managers can concentrate on strategy.	5. Figures may be subject to bias if junior managers either try to impress or set easily achievable targets (budgetary slack).
	6. Certain environments may preclude participation, e.g. sales manager may be faced with long-term contracts already agreed.

Recap of key aspects of Management Accounting: Budgeting

Basic methods of budgeting

Incremental (historic)

- Starts with previous period's budget or actual results and adds (or subtracts) an incremental amount to cover inflation and other known changes.
- Suitable for stable businesses, where costs are not expected to change significantly.
- There should be good cost control and limited discretionary costs.

Zero-based budgeting

- Requires cost element to be specifically justified, as though the activities to which the budget relates were being undertaken for the first time.
- Without approval, the budget allowance is zero.
- Suitable for allocating resources in areas were spend is discretionary.

Priority-based budgeting

- A competitively ranked listing of high to low priority discrete bids for "decision packages."
  - All activities are re-evaluated each time a budget is set.
  - Does not require a zero assumption.

Activity-based budgeting

- Preparing budgets using overhead costs from activity based costing methodology.

Flexed budgets

For variances to be meaningful and appropriate for use as decision-making tools, a **flexed budget** should be prepared to take into account the change between the budgeted levels of activity (sales and production) and the actual levels.

	Budget	Flexed budget	Actual
Sales volume	100 units	90 units	90 units
Sales value	£1,000	£900	£990
Variable costs	£500	£450	£495
Fixed costs	£200	£200	£210
Profit	£300	£250	£285

Flexible budgets

A **fixed** budget contains information on costs and revenue for one level of activity. A **flexible** budget shows the same information, but for a number of different levels of activity.

	Low	Normal	High
Activity level	80,000 units	100,000 units	120,000 units
Revenue	£3,200,000	£4,000,000	£4,800,000
Variable costs	£1,440,000	£1,800,000	£2,160,000
Fixed costs	£300,000	£300,000	£300,000
Profit	£1,460,000	£1,900,000	£2,340,000

A **flexible** budget model makes it possible to quickly amend the line items in the event of some unforeseen complication. For example, should sales volume suddenly drop, affecting the amount of generated revenue, the flexible format makes it easy to quickly change the amounts associated with specific line items to reflect the new set of circumstances.

The ability to quickly adjust a flexible budget to take into account changes in output levels or shifts in income means that a business can move quickly to meet the new circumstances. By contrast, a fixed budget, that is based on a single set of projections and allows no room for adjustments without going through a complicated approval process, wastes valuable time and money that could be used more efficiently.

Materials variances

1 Materials price variance

The material price variance is calculated compared to what we expected to pay, so that we can work out whether we have paid too much or too little for our materials.

We always use the **Purchased quantity** in the calculation and we compare the Actual price paid and the **Standard** (expected) price.

Formula:
Actual quantity purchased × Actual price V Actual quantity purchased × Standard price
Materials price variance   £X F/ A

We can also use what we call the Did and Should method to work out an answer.

x units did cost	£X
x units should have cost @ £x	£X
Variance	£X F/A

2 Materials Usage variance

The materials usage variance is calculated so that we can work out whether we have used too much or too little material to manufacture our goods in the period.

We always use the Used quantity of material in the calculation, and we compare the Actual amount of materials used with the Standard (expected) amount of materials that we should use to make the actual volume of goods in the period (the activity level).

> **Formula:**
>
> Actual quantity used × Standard price
> V
> Standard quantity used for actual production × Standard price
>
> Materials usage variance £X F/A

We can also use what we call the Did and Should method to work out an answer.

x units did use	x	kgs
x units should have used @ 2 sq metres per box	x	kgs
	x	kgs
Multiplied by the standard (expected) price	*£x	
So variance is	£X	

Labour variances

1 Labour rate variance

The labour rate variance is calculated so that we can work out whether or not we have paid the correct hourly rate to the direct labour employees. We always use the total hours paid and we compare the Actual hourly rate paid and the standard (expected) hourly rate.

Formula:
Actual labour hours paid × Actual rate V Actual labour hours paid × Standard rate
Labour rate variance   £X F/A

When calculating the labour rate variance we could again use what we call the Did and Should method to work out the answer.

x hours did cost	£X
x hours should have cost @ £X per hour	£X
Variance	£X

2 Labour efficiency variance

The labour efficiency variance is calculated so that we can work out whether we have used too much or too little labour to manufacture our goods in the period.

We always use the worked quantity of hours and we compare the actual number of hours worked and the standard (expected) number of hours that we should work to make the volume of goods in the period (the activity level).

> **Formula:**
>
> Actual hours worked × Standard rate
> V
> Standard hours worked for actual production × Standard rate
>
> Labour efficiency variance £X F/A

We can use the Did and Should method to calculate the labour efficiency also.

X units did use	X hours
X units should have used @ x minutes per box	X hours
	X hours
Multiplied by the standard (expected) rate	× £X per hour
so variance is	£X

3 Idle time variance

The idle time variance is calculated as the difference between the direct labour hours paid and the direct labour hours worked. It is a balancing figure and it is always adverse. It is always calculated using the standard (expected) hourly rate.

```
Actual hours paid × Standard rate
V
Actual hours worked × Standard rate
```

Hours paid for	X hours
Hours worked	X hours
	X hours
Multiplied by the standard (expected) rate	× £X per hour
so variance is	£X F / A

Interdependence of variances

The cause of a variance may affect another variance in a corresponding or opposite way.

For example, workers trying to improve productivity (favourable labour efficiency variance) might become careless and waste more material (adverse material usage variance).

Variance investigation

Variance calculations are just the starting point. Next, management need to decide which variances are worth investigating. To do this they will consider the following.

- How big is the variance?
  - Absolute size
  - Relative size as a % of standard
  - Overall trend.
- Is it favourable or adverse?
- Possible reasons for it
  - Planning errors
  - Measurement problems
  - Random factors
  - Operational issues.
- Controllability.
- Cost v benefit of investigation.
- Likelihood of a problem, based on past experience.
- The overall picture given by all the variances.

Management will seek to assign responsibility for the variances so they can be investigated further.

Reasons for variances

Variance		Possible causes
Materials:	Price	Bulk discounts
		Different suppliers/ Different materials
		Unexpected delivery costs
		Different buying procedures
	Usage	Different quality material
		Theft, obsolescence, deterioration
		Different quality of staff
		Different mix of material
		Different batch sizes and trim loss
Labour:	Rate	Different class of labour
		Excessive overtime
		Productivity bonuses
		National wage negotiations
		Union action

Variance		Possible causes
	Efficiency	Different levels of skill
		Different working conditions
		The learning effect
		Lack of supervision
		Works to rule
		Machine breakdowns
		Lack of material
		Lack of orders
		Strikes (if paid)
		Too long over coffee breaks
Overhead:	Price	Change in nature of overhead
		Unforeseen price changes
	Volume	Excessive idle time
		Increase in workforce

Recap of key aspects of Management Accounting: Budgeting

Performance indicators

The examiner has grouped these measures into four areas:

1 **Quality** indicators such as reject rates.
2 **Efficiency indicators,** such as the number of products made per labour hour, or idle time ratios.
3 **Capacity measures,** such as machine utilisation ratios (or 'asset utilisation' ratios).
4 **Simple financial measures** such as the average selling price, profit percentage of sales revenue, material cost of material per unit of purchase, labour rate per hour, cost per unit of production and sales and cost variances.

chapter 11

Recap of key aspects of Management Accounting: Decision and control

- Differences between absorption and marginal costing.
- MC and TAC – Summary.
- Breakeven analysis.
- Limiting factors.
- Standard costing.
- Variance analysis – overview.
- Materials variances.
- Labour variances.
- Variable overhead variances.
- Fixed overhead variances.
- Variance investigation.
- Performance measurement.
- Profitability ratios.
- Liquidity ratios.
- Working capital ratios.
- Investor ratio.
- Additional ratios.
- The balanced scorecard.
- Lifecycle costing.
- Target costing.
- Activity Based Costing (ABC).

Differences between absorption and marginal costing

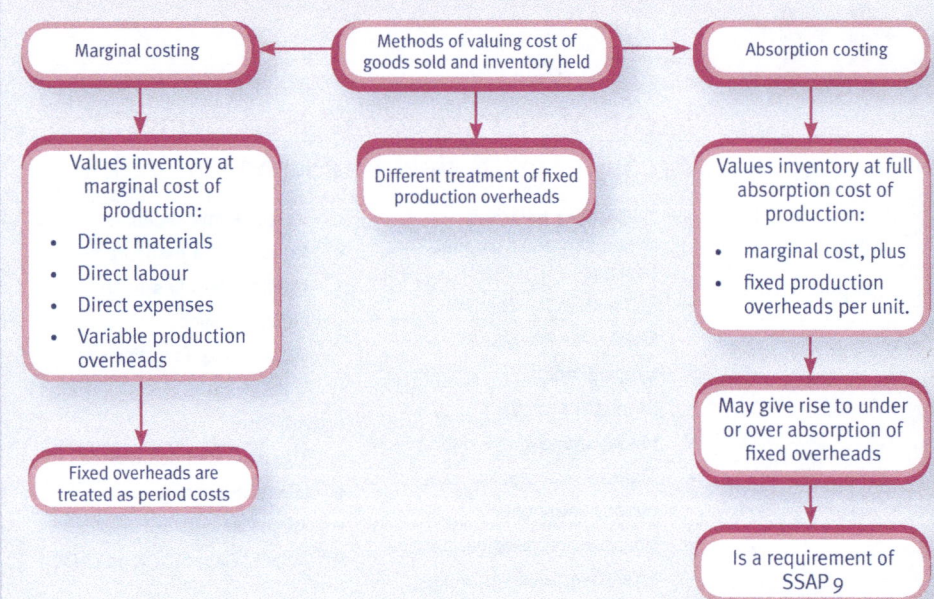

MC and TAC – summary

Marginal costing (MC)

In marginal costing, units of inventory are valued incorporating only variable production costs.

- More consistent with short term decision making techniques as most focus on contribution.
- Can also be simpler as fixed costs do not have to be apportioned.
- Cannot boost profit simply by making more units (unlike TAC).

Total absorption costing

In absorption costing, inventories are valued by incorporating all production costs, both fixed and variable.

- Suitable for financial reporting.
- Suitable for 'full cost plus' pricing, ensuring that all costs are covered.
- Profit fluctuates less when faced with seasonal trade.

Overhead absorption is achieved by means of a predetermined Overhead Absorption Rate (OAR).

Breakeven analysis

Breakeven point

- Volume of sales at which neither a profit nor a loss is made
- $$\frac{\text{Fixed cost}}{\text{Contribution/unit}}$$

Example
A micro hi-fi system sells for £160. It has a variable cost of £70 per unit, and fixed costs are £378,000 per annum.

$$\text{Breakeven point} = \frac{\text{Fixed cost}}{\text{Contribution per unit}}$$

$$= \frac{£378{,}000}{£(160-70)}$$

$$= \frac{£378{,}000}{£90}$$

$$= 4{,}200 \text{ units}$$

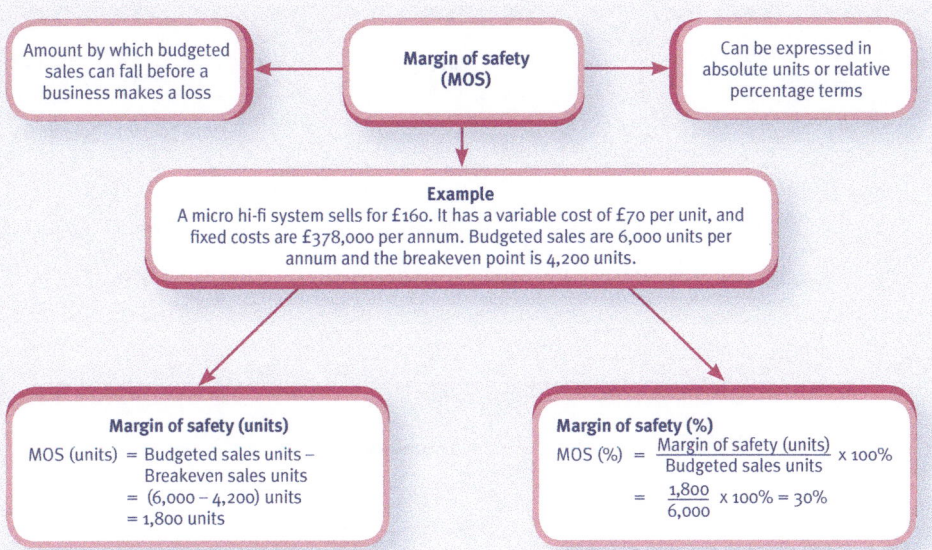

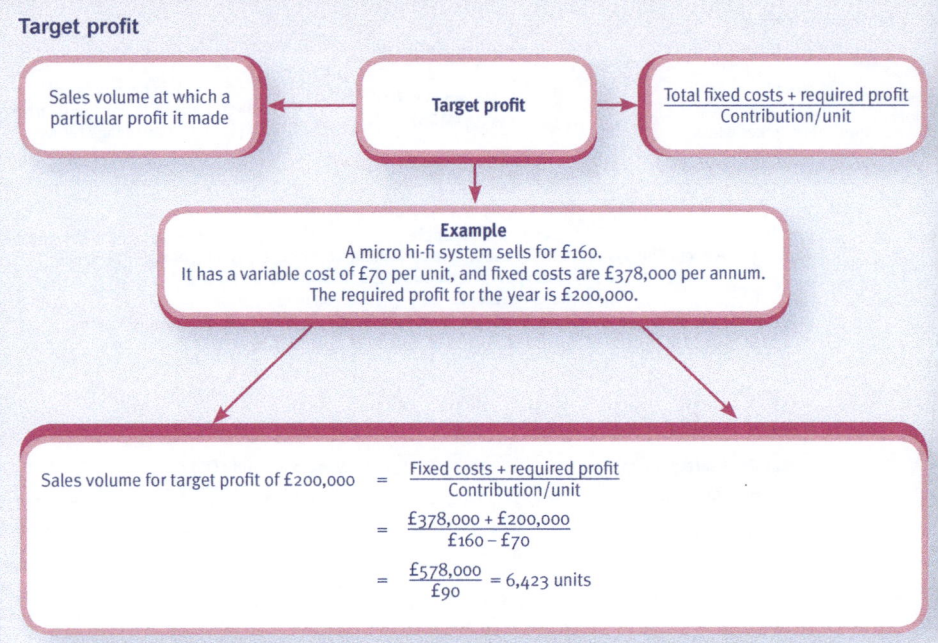

Limiting factors

Definition

Key factor analysis is a technique used when we have one resource that is in scarce supply and we can make more than one type of product using that resource. Key factor analysis determines how to use this resource in such a way that profits are maximised.

Approach to key factor analysis

(1) Determine the limiting factor or key factor that is in scarce supply

(2) Calculate the contribution per unit generated by each product

(3) Calculate the contribution per unit of scarce resource for each product

$$\frac{\text{Contribution per unit}}{\text{Number of units of scarce resource needed}}$$

(4) Select the product with the highest contribution per unit of scarce resource and make this first

Standard costing

Objective is to control the business:

1. Set up standard costs, prepare budgets and set targets.
2. Measure actual performance.
3. Compare actual v budget via variances.
4. Investigate reasons for differences and take action.

Types of standard:

- Ideal standards are based on optimal operating conditions with maximum efficiency and are usually unobtainable under normal conditions.
- Attainable standards are based on existing operating conditions.
- Basic standards are left unchanged from one period to another.
- Current standards are adjusted for each period.

Standard cost card

The standard cost card is a schedule that gives the standard costs that a unit of a product **should** incur.

Example

	£
Materials (2kg at £3 per kg)	6
Labour (0.5 hours at £18 per hour)	9
Overheads (0.5 hours at £20 per hour)	10
Total standard cost per unit	25

Advantages of standard costing

- Comparison of actual costs to standard enables management to judge performance.
- Facilitates 'management by exception' – i.e. concentrate on investigating the most significant variances.
- Simplifies bookkeeping if Inventories are valued at standard.

Disadvantages of standard costing

- Standards can quickly become out of date.
- Establishing standards, monitoring of system and investigation of variances is costly.
- Unrealistic standards can demotivate staff.

Variance analysis – overview

Comparing like with like

When calculating variances it is vital that you compare like with like.

For each cost we compare the actual cost with how much it **should** have cost to produce the same actual level of output:

Actual cost

↕ Variance

Standard cost of actual production

Materials variances

Materials Price variance

This is based on the actual quantity of materials purchased:

Materials purchased did cost

Actual quantity purchased × Actual price = X

Materials purchased should have cost

Actual quantity purchased × Standard price = X

} Price variance

Materials Usage variance

Quantity actually used at SP

Actual quantity used × Standard price = X

Quantity that should have been used at SP

Standard quantity used* × Standard price = X

} Usage variance

* i.e. quantity that should have been used to make actual output.

Reasons for variances

Price Variance

1. Wrong standards.
2. Lower/higher quality material.
3. Different supplier.
4. Good/poor purchasing.
5. External factors (inflation, exchange rates etc).

Usage Variance

1. Wrong standards.
2. Lower/higher quality of material.
3. Lower/higher quality of labour.
4. Theft.

Recap of key aspects of Management Accounting: Decision and control

Labour variances

Labour Rate variance

Hours paid did cost
Actual hours × Actual rate = X
Hours paid should have cost
Actual hours × Standard rate = X
} Rate variance

Labour Efficiency variance

Hours actually paid at SR
Actual hours × Standard rate = X
Hours that should have been paid at SR
Standard hours* × Standard rate = X
} Efficiency variance

* i.e. hours firm should have worked to make the actual output

Reasons for variances

Rate Variance

1. Wrong standards.
2. Wage inflation.
3. Lower/higher skilled employees.
4. Unplanned overtime or bonuses.

Efficiency variance

1. Wrong standards.
2. Lower/higher morale.
3. Lower/higher skilled employees.
4. Lower/higher quality of material.

Variable overhead variances

Variable overhead expenditure variance
Hours worked did cost
Actual hours worked × Actual rate = X
Hours worked should have cost   } Expenditure variance
Actual hours worked × Standard rate = X

Variable overhead efficiency variance
Hours actually worked at SR
Actual hours worked × Standard rate = X
Hours that should have been worked at SR   } Efficiency variance
Standard hours*   × Standard rate = X

* i.e. hours firm should have worked to make the actual output

Reasons for variances

Expenditure Variance

1. Wrong standards.
2. Rate inflation.

Efficiency variance

1. Wrong standards.
2. Lower/higher morale.
3. Lower/higher skilled employees.
4. Lower/higher quality of material.

Recap of key aspects of Management Accounting: Decision and control

Fixed overhead variances

Definition

The total fixed overhead variance is the difference between the actual fixed overhead, and the absorbed fixed overhead.

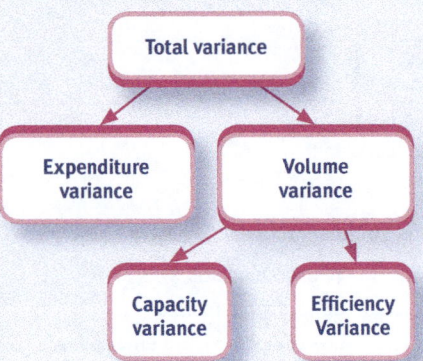

Fixed overhead expenditure variance (MC and TAC)

Actual fixed overheads = X
Budgeted fixed overheads = X
} Expenditure variance

Note: this is the original budget unadjusted for differences in output.

Fixed overhead volume variance (TAC only)

The volume variance is the difference between the budgeted overhead absorbed and the actual overhead absorbed.

Budgeted production × Standard cost per unit = X
Actual production × Standard cost per unit = X
} Volume var.

Fixed overhead capacity and efficiency variances (TAC only)

The volume variance can be split into capacity and efficiency variances. To do this you need to have a standard fixed cost rate per labour hour:

Standard rate per hour

$$= \frac{\text{Budgeted fixed costs}}{\text{Budgeted hours}}$$

The variances are:

Budgeted hours	x Standard rate per hour	= X	} Capacity var.
Actual hours worked	x Standard rate per hour	= X	
			} Efficiency var.
Standard hours for actual production	x Standard rate per hour	= X	

Reasons for fixed overhead variances

Fixed Overhead Expenditure Variance (MC and TAC)

The expenditure variance is the simplest fixed overhead variance and simply compares the original budgeted figure with actual. The variance will be due to poor budgeting or to a price rise.

e.g. rent increased by landlord.

Fixed Overhead Volume Variance (TAC)

The volume variance is due to the volume of production changing. A favourable (adverse) variance reflects the fact that more (less) units were made than planned. This could be due to:

- Poor budgeting.
- Labour efficiency.
- Availability of resources (e.g. shortage of materials).

Fixed Overhead Capacity Variance (TAC)

The capacity variance is due to the number of labour hours worked changing. A favourable (adverse) variance reflects the fact that more (less) hours were worked than originally planned, due to:

- Poor budgeting.
- Overtime.
- Staff sickness.
- Machine breakdown.

Fixed Overhead Efficiency Variance (TAC)

The efficiency variance is due to the efficiency of labour and is thus due to the same factors as the labour efficiency variance above.

If the labour efficiency variance is favourable (adverse) then the fixed overhead efficiency variance will also be favourable (adverse). (This is assuming absorption is based on labour hours.)

Variance investigation

Variance calculations are just the starting point. Next, management need to decide which variances are worth investigating. To do this they will consider the following.

- How big is the variance?
  - Absolute size.
  - Relative size as a % of standard.
  - Overall trend.
- Is it favourable or adverse?
- Possible reasons for it.
  - Planning errors.
  - Measurement problems.
  - Random factors.
  - Operational issues.
- Controllability.
- Cost v benefit of investigation.
- Likelihood of a problem, based on past experience.
- The overall picture given by all the variances.

Management will seek to assign responsibility for the variances so they can be investigated further.

Recap of key aspects of Management Accounting: Decision and control

CBA focus

Performance appraisal is a very important topic. Two styles of task are commonplace:

Some tasks ask you to assess the organisation using ratios and other KPIs.

Some tasks give some new circumstances and require you to produce forecasts/revised ratios based on those changes.

Try to relate your comments to any details given in the scenario:

e.g. a switch to more expensive materials could explain changes in margins and quality.

Try to discuss both financial and non-financial indicators.

Performance measurement

An effective system of performance measurement is critical if the business is to be controlled.

Performance indicators can be:

- quantitative (i.e. expressed in numbers); or
- qualitative (i.e. not expressed in numbers). For example, satisfied/not satisfied or grade poor to excellent.

The 3Es

- **Economy** is the degree to which low prices were paid for the inputs of the business.
- **Effectiveness** is the degree to which the business objectives have been met.
- **Efficiency** is the relationship between inputs and outputs achieved, i.e. that as few inputs as possible have been used to achieve a particular output level of the desired quality.

Benchmarking

Need a suitable basis for comparison.

- Internal benchmarking. For example, by division.
- Competitive benchmarking.
- Activity (or process) benchmarking.
- Generic benchmarking – look at conceptually similar processes.

Profitability ratios

Return on capital employed (ROCE)

Capital employed is normally measured as non-current assets plus current assets less current liabilities and represents the long-term investment in the business. It is also measured as owners' capital plus long-term liabilities. Return on capital employed is frequently regarded as the best measure of profitability.

$$ROCE = \frac{\text{Profit before interest and taxation (PBIT)}}{\text{Capital employed}} \times 100\%$$

Note that the profit before interest is used, because the loan capital rewarded by that interest is included in capital employed.

Recap of key aspects of Management Accounting: Decision and control

A low return on capital employed (assets used) is caused by either a low profit margin or a low asset turnover or both. This can be seen by breaking down the primary ROCE ratio into its two components: profit margin and asset turnover.

$$ROCE = \frac{PBIT}{Capital\ employed}$$

$$= \frac{PBIT}{Revenue} \times \frac{Revenue}{Capital\ employed}$$

$$= Profit\ margin \times Asset\ turnover$$

Profit margin (on revenue)

$$Profit\ margin = \frac{Profit\ before\ interest\ and\ taxation}{Revenue} \times 100\%$$

A low margin indicates low selling prices or high costs or both.

Asset turnover

This will show the extent to which a company is utilising its assets to generate turnover:

$$Asset\ turnover = \frac{Revenue}{Capital\ employed}$$

A low turnover shows that a company is not generating a sufficient volume of business for the size of the asset base. This may be remedied by increasing sales or by disposing of some of the assets or both.

Gross profit margin

$$Gross\ profit\ margin = \frac{Gross\ profit}{Revenue} \times 100\%$$

The gross profit margin focuses on the trading account. A low margin could indicate selling prices too low or cost of sales too high.

Liquidity ratios

Current ratio

This indicates the extent to which the claims of short-term payables are covered by assets that are expected to be converted to cash.

$$\text{Current ratio} = \frac{\text{Current assets}}{\text{Current liabilities}}$$

Quick ratio (Acid test ratio)

This is calculated in the same way as the current ratio except that inventories are excluded from current assets, since they may not be converted into cash very quickly.

$$\text{Quick ratio} = \frac{\text{Current assets} - \text{inventory}}{\text{Current liabilities}}$$

This ratio is a much better test of immediate solvency.

Working capital ratios

Receivables collection period (Receivable days)

This is computed by dividing the receivables by the average daily sales to determine the number of days' sales held in receivables.

$$\text{Receivables collection period} = \frac{\text{Trade receivables}}{\text{Credit sales}} \times 365 \text{ days}$$

A long average collection period probably indicates poor credit control. If a company offers standard terms to its credit customers (e.g. 30 days credit), then the actual period of credit taken can be compared to the standard period.

Recap of key aspects of Management Accounting: Decision and control

Payables payment period

This is computed by dividing the payables by the average daily credit purchases to determine the number of days purchases held in payables. This tells us how long we are taking to pay our creditors. Too long a payment period may mean that they refuse to sell us goods in the future.

$$\text{Payables payment period} = \frac{\text{Trade payables}}{\text{Credit purchases}} \times 365 \text{ days}$$

Inventory holding period

This ratio indicates whether inventory levels are justified in relation to sales.

$$\text{Inventory holding period} = \frac{\text{Inventory}}{\text{Cost of sales}} \times 365 \text{ days}$$

Investor ratio

Gearing ratio

$$\text{Gearing ratio} = \text{Debt} / \text{Equity} \times 100$$

This ratio measures the proportion of assets invested in the business that are financed by borrowing.

A high gearing ratio means that the business is financed by a lot of debt, which can be dangerous. High levels of interest will be payable which the company may not be able to afford in a year of low profit.

Additional ratios

Manufacturing productivity

Activity ratio =
$$\frac{\text{Standard hours for actual production}}{\text{Budgeted hours}} \times 100\%$$

Capacity ratio =
$$\frac{\text{Actual hours worked}}{\text{Budgeted hours}} \times 100\%$$

Efficiency ratio =
$$\frac{\text{Standard hours for actual production}}{\text{Actual hours worked}} \times 100\%$$

Note: Efficiency ratio x Capacity ratio = Activity ratio.

The formula for these three ratios will be given in the assessment if required.

Adding value

Added value = sales price – cost of bought-in goods and services.

Others, depending on the scenario:

Output per employee.

Sales per employee.

Number of defects.

Delivery time to customer.

Rooms cleaned per hour.

The balanced scorecard

From strategic objectives to performance indicators

Chapter 11

The balanced scorecard performance management system

	Financial perspective	Customer perspective	Internal business process perspective	Innovation and learning perspective
Strategic objective	Shareholder satisfaction	Customer satisfaction	Manufacturing excellence	New product innovation
CSF	Grow shareholder wealth	Achieve preferred supplier status	State-of-the-art process plant	Successful new product development
KPIs	• ROCE • Growth %	• Number of customer partnerships	• Cycle times • Unit cost • % yield	• % of revenues represented by new products

Lifecycle costing

All products go through lifecycles

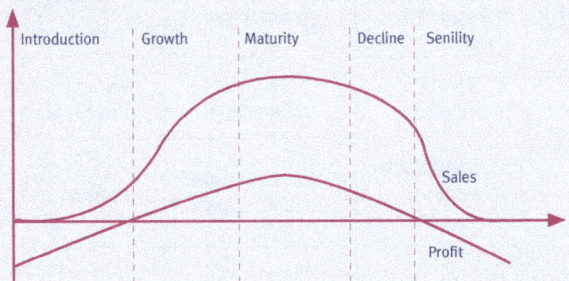

As shown by the difference between the revenue and cost curves, the pattern of costs over the lifecycle does not match that of revenue.

In particular, there will be high development costs during the introduction stage.

Traditional financial accounting has the following problems in this respect:

- It will look at the profit in a particular year, rather than assessing profitability over the whole lifecycle.

- Research costs are often written off in the year in which they are incurred rather than matching against (later) revenue.

Target costing

Many firms operate a 'cost-plus' pricing system, where the selling price of a product is calculated by adding a mark-up to the production cost.

Target costing is the reverse of this process:

1. The firm estimates the likely product price by looking at market conditions, competition, etc.

2. A target mark-up % is deducted from the price to give a target cost.

3. Production then sees if it can produce the product at the cost required.

Example

R plc makes fridges. The current cost per unit is £100 and R sells them for £200, a mark-up of 100%. Due to increased competition, R feels that a selling price of £160 would be more competitive.

Assuming the mark up of 100% is still required, calculate the target cost.

Solution

Target price = £160

Target cost = 160 x 100/200 = £80

The production department needs to try to save £20 per unit on cost.

Activity Based Costing (ABC)

Step 1 Identify major activities.

Step 2 Identify appropriate cost drivers.

Step 3 Collect costs into pools based upon the activities (note: this is usually done for you in a question/task)

Step 4 Charge costs to units of production based on cost driver rate.

$$\text{Cost driver rate} = \frac{\text{Cost pool}}{\text{Level of cost driver}}$$

Examples of cost drivers

- Machine costs could be charged using machine hours.
- Quality control costs could be charged using number of inspections.
- Set-up costs could be charged using number of set-ups.

Benefits and Limitations of ABC

Benefits	Limitations
1. Provides more accurate product line costings.	1. Little evidence to date that ABC improves corporate profitability.
2. Is flexible enough to analyse costs by cost objects other than products, such as processes, areas of managerial responsibility and customers.	2. ABC information is historic and internally orientated and therefore lacks direct relevance for future strategic decisions.
3. Provides meaningful financial (periodic cost driver rates) and non-financial (periodic cost driver volume) measures.	3. Practical problems such as cost driver selection.
4. Aids identification and understanding of cost behaviour and thus has the potential to improve cost estimation.	
5. Provides a more logical, acceptable and comprehensible basis for costing work.	

Recap of key aspects of Management Accounting: Decision and control

Index

Index

A
AAT Code of Professional Ethics 67
Accounting function 7
Accruals 66
Activity Based Costing (ABC) 116
Additional ratios 111
Areas of interaction 9
Asset 65
Asset turnover 36, 108

B
Basic methods of budgeting 78
Benchmarking 107
Bottom-up budgeting 76
Breakeven analysis 92
Breakeven point 92

C
Cash and cheques 24
Changeover methods 51
Comparability 64
Comparative information 66
Confidentiality 55
Consistency of presentation 66
Contingency controls 34
Control mechanisms 6
Cost-benefit analysis 49

D
Data Security 29
Department 9

E
Efficiency ratios 37
Equity 65
Ethics 54
Expenses 65

F
Faithful representation 64
Financial statements 14
Flexible budgets 80
Fraud 44
FRS Interpretation Committee (IFRS IC) 10

G
Going concern 66
Gross profit margin 36, 108

Index

I
IAS 1 Presentation of Financial Statements 66
IASB framework 64
IFRS Advisory Council (IFRS AC): 10
IFRS Foundation 10, 62
Implementing changes 50
Income 65
Information systems controls 28
Intangible benefits 49
Intangible costs 49
Integrity 55
Integrity controls 31
Interdependence of variances 85
Internal audit 20
Internal control 18
International Accounting Standards Board (IASB) 10
Interpreting financial information 38
Interpreting ratios 38
Investor ratios 37, 110

J
Justification of change 49

K
Key factor analysis 95
Key ratios 71

L
Labour variances 83, 100
Legal framework 63
Lifecycle costing 114
Limitations of ratio analysis 39, 74
Limiting factors 95
Linking ratios and control problems 40
Liquidity ratios 109
Long-term solvency 37

M
Management accounting 15
Management reports 15
Marginal costing 91
Margin of safety 93
Materiality and aggregation 66
Materials variances 81, 99

N
NPV 49

Index

O
Objectivity 55
Offsetting 66
Operating profit margin 36
Operational security 29

P
Payback 49
Payroll 23
Performance indicators 88
Performance measurement 106
Physical security 29
Present obligation of the entity 65
Professional behaviour 55
Professional competence and due care 55
Profitability ratios 107
Profit margin (on revenue) 108
Purchases cycle 21

Q
Quick ratio (Acid test ratio) 109

R
Reasons for variances 87
Regulations affecting the accounting function 10
Relevance 64
Resistance to change 50
Return on capital employed (ROCE) 36, 107

S
Safeguards 68
Sales cycle 22
Segregation of duties 25
Short-term liquidity 37
Software security 29
Standard cost card 96
Standard costing 96
Statement of cash flow 14
Statement of changes in equity 14
Statement of financial position 14
Statement of other comprehensive income 14
Statement of profit or loss 14
Stewardship 14
Sustainability 57
Sustainability and the accounting system 59

SWOT 49
Systems 11
Systems integrity 33

T
Tangible benefits 49
Tangible costs 49
Target costing 115
Target profit 94
The 3Es 106
The accounting function 7
The balanced scorecard 112
Threats 68
Timeliness 64
Top-down budgeting 76
Total absorption costing 91
Transportataion process 11
Types of standard 96

U
Understandability 64
User groups 16
Uses of ratios 70

V
Variable overhead variances 101
Variance analysis 98
Variance investigation 86, 105
Verifiability 64

W
Working capital ratios 109

Index

CONTENTS

		Reference to Study Text chapter	Page Number
A guide to the assessment			1
Chapter 1	The business organisation	1	5
Chapter 2	The legal framework for companies and partnerships	2	15
Chapter 3	Business stakeholders' interactions and needs	3	23
Chapter 4	Organisational structure and governance	4	31
Chapter 5	The role of the finance function	5	43
Chapter 6	Risk and risk management	6	51
Chapter 7	External analysis – the PESTLE model	7	59
Chapter 8	The micro-economic environment	8	61
Chapter 9	Sustainability	8	69
Chapter 10	Professional ethics in accounting and business	8	75
Chapter 11	Money laundering	8	81
Chapter 12	Technology affecting business and finance	8	89
Chapter 13	Data protection, information security and cybersecurity	8	99

Business Awareness

Chapter 14	Information and Big Data	8	103
Chapter 15	Visualising information	8	107
Index			I.1

Preface

These Pocket Notes contain the key things that you need to know for the exam, presented in a unique visual way that makes revision easy and effective.

Written by experienced lecturers and authors, these Pocket Notes break down content into manageable chunks to maximise your concentration.

Quality and accuracy are of the utmost importance to us so if you spot an error in any of our products, please send an email to mykaplanreporting@kaplan.com with full details, or follow the link to the feedback form in MyKaplan.

Our Quality Co-ordinator will work with our technical team to verify the error and take action to ensure it is corrected in future editions.

Business Awareness

A guide to the assessment

A guide to the assessment

The assessment

BUAW is the business awareness unit on the Diploma in Accounting qualification.

Examination

Business Awareness is assessed by means of a computer-based assessment. The CBA will last for 2 hours 30 minutes and consist of 7 tasks. Some tasks will require extended (human-marked) responses.

In any one assessment, students may not be assessed on all content, or on the full depth or breadth of a piece of content. The content assessed may change over time to ensure validity of assessment, but all assessment criteria will be tested over time.

Learning outcomes & weighting

1. Understand business types, structures and governance, and the legal framework in which they operate — 25%

2. Understand the impact of the external and internal environment on businesses, their performance and decisions — 20%

3. Understand how businesses and accountants comply with principles of professional ethics — 20%

4. Understand the impact of new technologies in accounting and the risks associated with data security — 15%

5. Communicate information to stakeholders — 20%

Total — 100%

A guide to the assessment

Pass mark

To pass a unit assessment, students need to achieve a mark of 70% or more.

This unit contributes 15% of the total amount required for the Diploma in Accounting qualification.

A guide to the assessment

chapter 1

The business organisation

- The need for organisation and its types.
- Not for profit organisations.
- Services vs. manufacturing organisations.
- Separation of ownership and control.
- Types of funding.
- Equity and debt.

The need for organisation and its types

Organisations are social arrangements for the controlled performance of collective goals

- Two or more people working together in a structured way Duties and responsibilities being assigned to each individual
- Organisations use systems (e.g. swiping in when entering office) and procedures (e.g. cash handling rules) to regulate staff behaviour
- All organisations pursue certain goals, these are considered to be over and above individual aspirations

Organisations exist:

- to satisfy social needs
- to overcome the individuals' limitations
- to enable individuals to specialise
- to save time through joint effort
- to pool knowledge and ideas
- to pool expertise
- to provide synergy.

Organisational types

Organisations can differ depending on their areas of activity, geographical spread of operations, size etc. However the two main types of the organisation can be classified:

1 by profit orientation

   profit-seeking organisations:
   seek to maximise the wealth of their owners
   (e.g. commercial companies)

   not-for-profit organisations (NFPs):
   seek to satisfy the needs of their members, profit is no longer a primary objective
   (e.g. schools, hospitals).

2 by ownership/control

   public sector:

   provision of basic governmental services
   (e.g. police, education, healthcare)

   private sector limited liability
   (Ltds and plcs)

   - partnerships
   - clubs
   - cooperatives owned by people who buy or use their services.

The business organisation

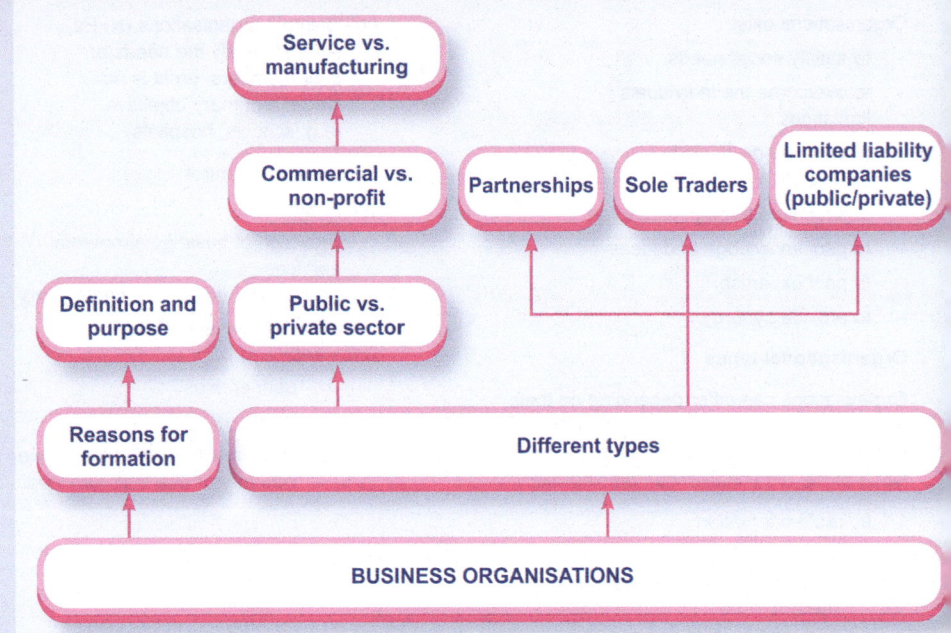

Not for profit organisations

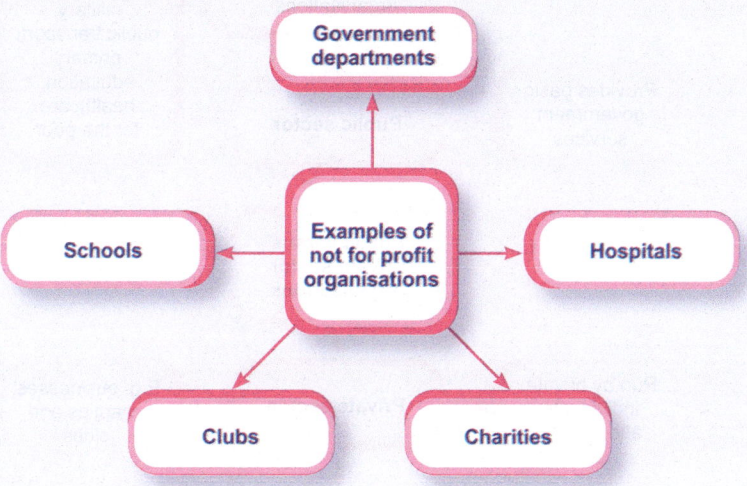

The business organisation

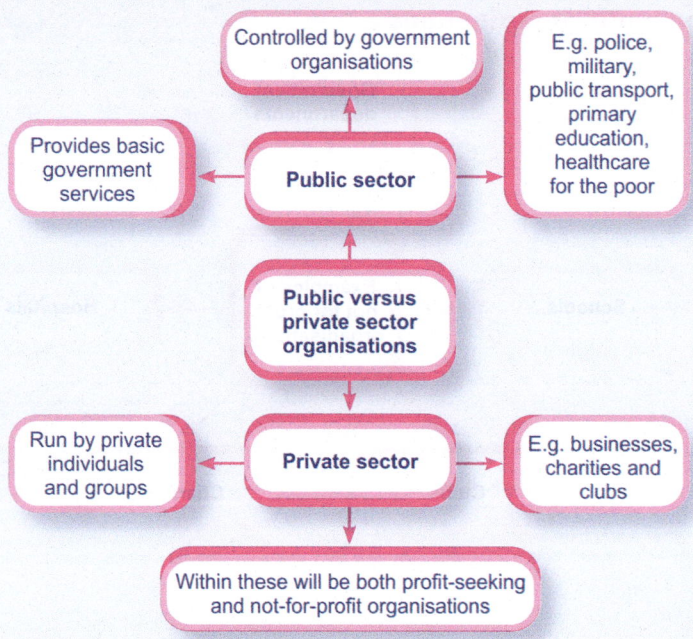

Services vs. manufacturing organisations

Differences can be remembered using the SHIP mnemonic

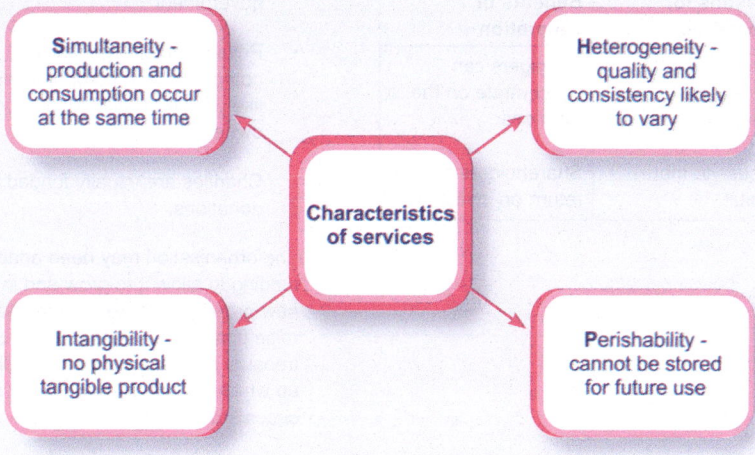

Separation of ownership and control

Reasons for separation	Benefits of separation
Specialist management expertise	Managers can concentrate on the business
Access to more capital	Shareholders earn a return on investment

Types of funding

- Public sector organisations will tend to raise money from the central government.

- Private sector organisations, such as companies and co-operatives, will most likely have to raise funds from their owners.

- Charities are usually funded by donations.

The organisation may need additional funding to allow it to grow and invest in new projects. It therefore may need to raise finance from external sources. The treasury and finance function will weigh up which source of finance best suits the circumstances of the business.

Equity and debt

Debt

This involves borrowing cash from a third party and promising to repay them at a later date. Normally the company will also have to pay interest on the amount borrowed.

Advantages:

- interest payments allowable against tax
- does not change ownership of the organisation
- tends to be cheaper to service than equity as it is often secured against assets of the company and take priority over equity in the event of the business being liquidated.

Equity

This involves selling a stake in the business in order to raise cash.

Advantages:

- no minimum level of dividend that must be paid to shareholders. Interest payments on debt finance must be paid each year
- a bank will normally require security on the company's assets before it will offer a loan. Some companies may lack quality assets to offer, making equity more attractive as it does not require security.

The business organisation

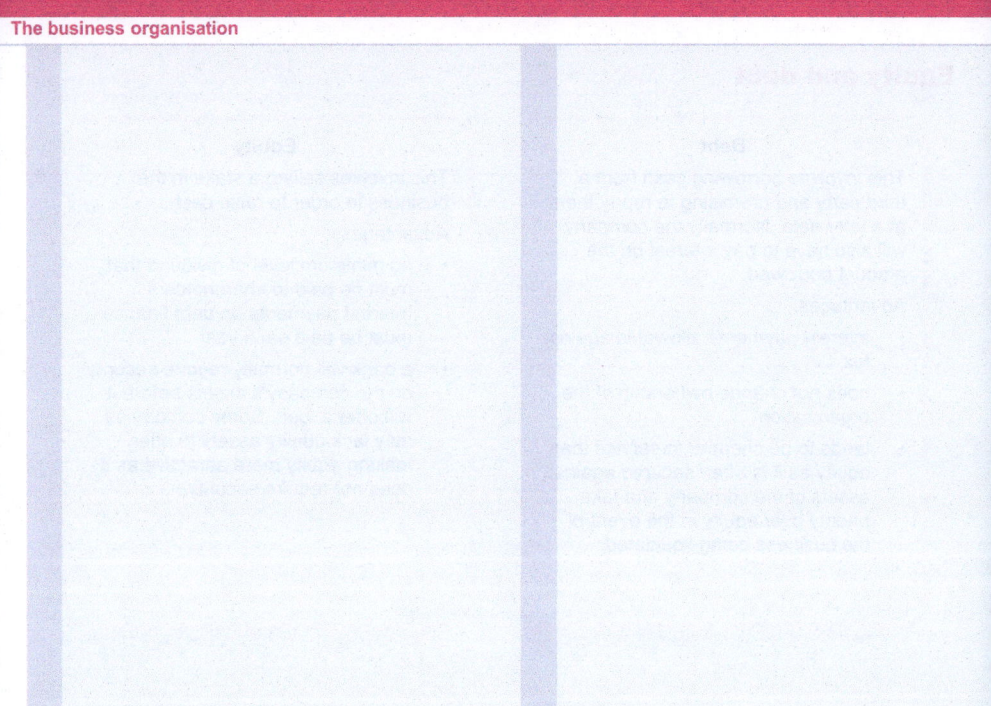

chapter 2

The legal framework for companies and partnerships

- Not for profit organisations.
- Directors.
- Shareholders.
- Unlimited liability partnerships.

The legal framework for companies and partnerships

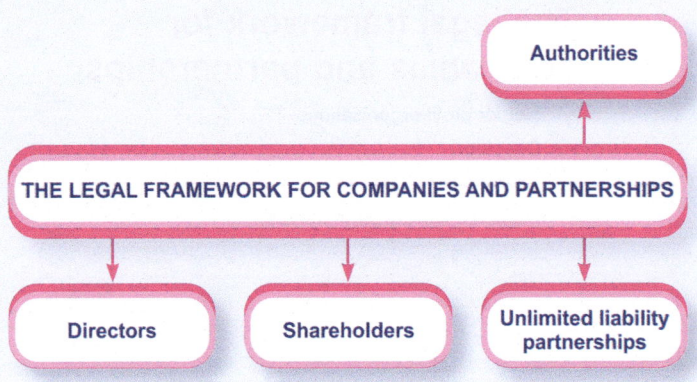

Not for profit organisations

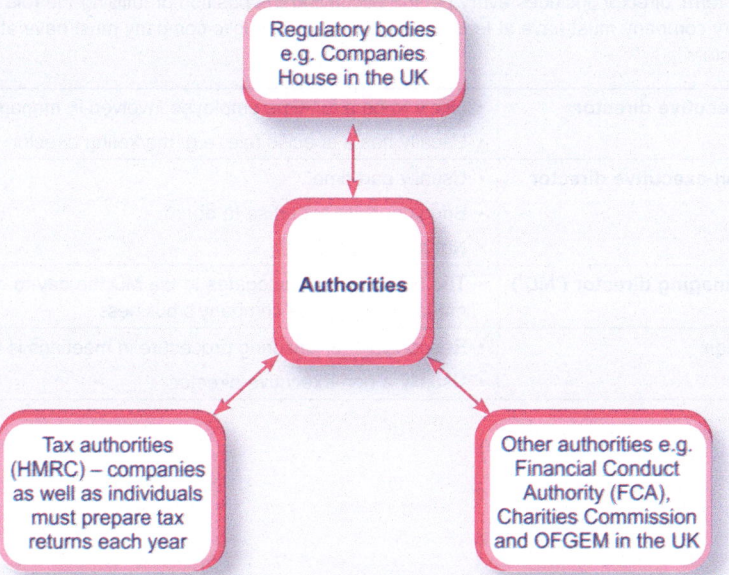

Directors

The term 'director' includes every person occupying the position or fulfilling the role of director: Every company must have at least one director and a public company must have at least two directors.

Executive director	• Likely to be a full-time employee involved in management.
	• Usually has a specific role, e.g. marketing director.
Non-executive director	• Usually part-time.
	• Brings outside expertise to board.
	• Not an employee.
Managing director ('MD')	• The board usually delegates to the MD the day-to-day management of the company's business.
Chair	• Responsible for ensuring procedure in meetings is followed.
	• Usually a non-executive director.

Directors duties

- To promote the success of the company.
- To act within powers.
- To exercise independent judgment.
- To exercise reasonable care and diligence.
- To avoid conflicts of interest.
- Not to accept benefits from third parties.
- To declare an interest in a proposed transaction or arrangement.
- To approve the financial statements and ensure that they show a true and fair view.

The legal framework for companies and partnerships

Shareholders

The shareholders have the right:

- To be sent a copy of annual accounts and reports.
- To require the directors to call a general meeting, and to attend general meetings.
- To receive dividends.
- To inspect company information.
- To vote on certain company affairs – subject to their class of shares and the articles of association.
- To be issued with a share certificate within two months of their shares being allotted.
- To inspect directors' service contracts.

Unlimited liability partnerships

Definition

A partnership describes 'the relationship that subsists between persons carrying on a business in common with a view to profit'.

A partnership is not a separate legal entity, and each partner has full personal liability for the partnership debts (liabilities).

When joint owners of a business are mutually responsible for the company's debt and liabilities and their personal liability isn't capped, this is known as an unlimited liability partnership.

An unlimited liability partnership, also known as a general partnership, is the default form of partnership. A partnership is often referred to as a firm.

- Partners all have unlimited personal liability: they are fully liable for any business debts. Third parties sue the partners, not the partnership as this is not a separate legal entity. The partners' liability is referred to as 'joint and several'. A third party can sue all the partners jointly, or can sue one partner individually.

- Owners may choose to trade as an unlimited partnership if they do not want to publicly file financial reports and annual accounts.

- Unlimited liability is suited to a business where the risk of insolvency is extremely low.

Goodwill

Goodwill is defined as 'the amount by which the fair value of the net assets of the partnership exceeds the carrying amount of the net assets'.

In simple terms, 'fair value' can be thought of as being the same as 'market value'.

- Goodwill arises due to factors such as reputation, location, market position, expertise and customer base.

- When a new partner joins a partnership they will not be entitled to any goodwill created by the old partnership. So the goodwill value at that point needs to be allocated to the old partners.

- A person joining a partnership will normally be expected to contribute capital to the partnership. A partner leaving a partnership would want to withdraw their capital (which will include any goodwill accumulated to the date of departure).

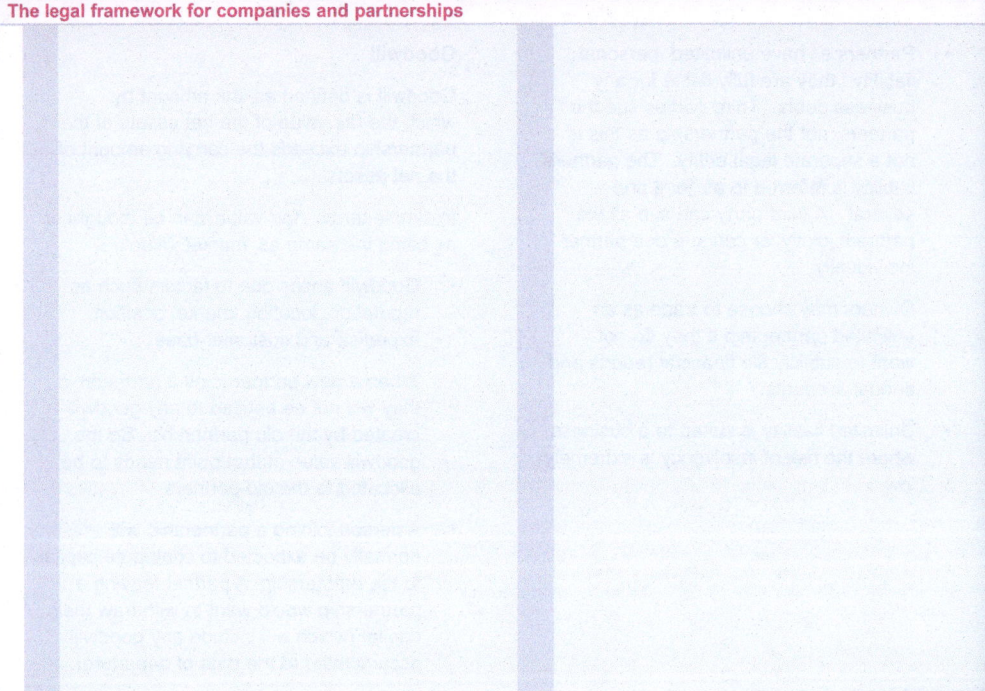

chapter 3

Business stakeholders' interactions and needs

- Stakeholders.
  - Connected.
  - Internal.
  - External.

Business stakeholders' interactions and needs

A **stakeholder** is an individual or group who has an interest in what the organisation does, or who affects, or can be affected by, the organisation's actions.

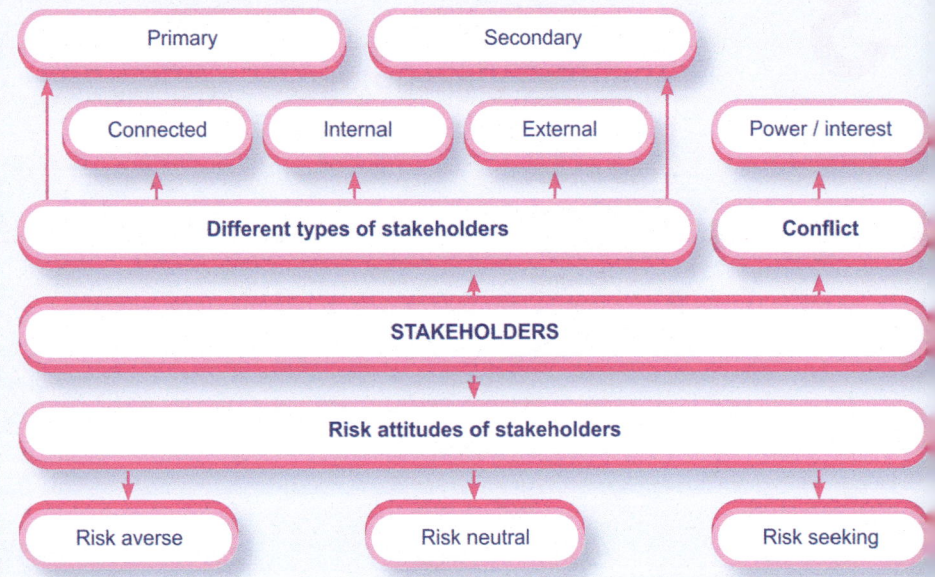

Stakeholders

Business stakeholders' interactions and needs

There are **three categories** of stakeholder.

Internal
internal parties involved in corporate governance e.g. employees and managers

Connected
invest in, or have dealings with, the firm e.g. shareholders, customers, suppliers

External
no direct link to the firm e.g. local community, government

Each stakeholder group has different needs and expectations in relation to the organisation.

Conflicts

An organisation can have many different stakeholders, all with different needs. Inevitably, the needs of some stakeholders will come into conflict with the needs of others.

Some of the most common conflicts include:

Stakeholders	Conflict
Employees versus managers	Jobs/wages versus profit-linked bonus (improved by cost efficiency)
Customers versus shareholders	Product quality/service levels versus profits/dividends
General public versus shareholders	Effect on the environment versus profit/dividends
Managers versus shareholders	Independence versus growth

Business stakeholders' interactions and needs

If an organisation is having difficulty deciding who the dominant stakeholder is, it can use **Mendelow's power-interest matrix**.

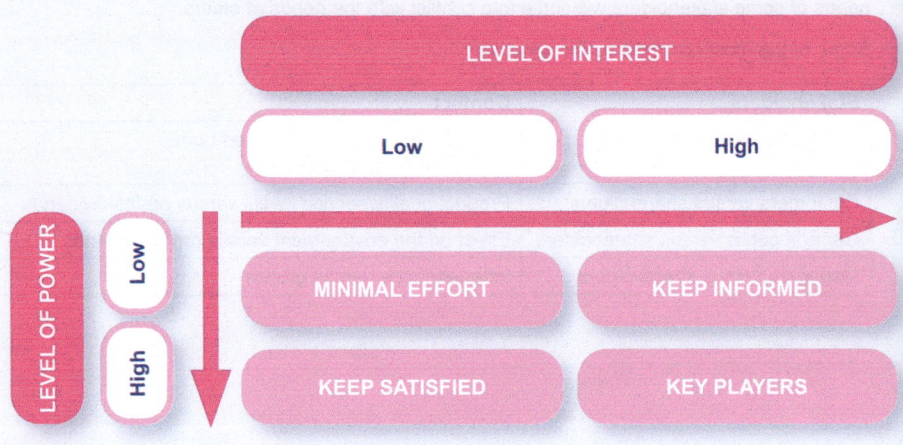

Managers need to consider the needs of as many stakeholders as possible when making decisions. This means that nearly every decision becomes a compromise.

Attitudes to risk

It is important to understand the tolerance levels of the stakeholders in relation to various factors including cost, quality, etc.

It is also important to accept that not all stakeholders will have the same attitude towards risk.

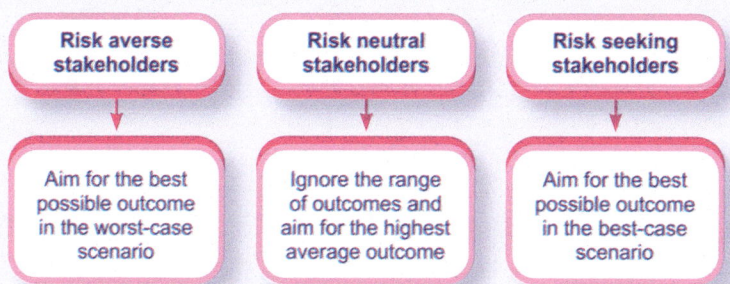

Business stakeholders' interactions and needs

chapter 4

Organisational structure and governance

- Entrepreneurial.
- Functional/departmental structure.
- Divisional/product structure.
- Divisions based on geographical areas.
- Matrix structure.
- Tall and flat organisations.
- Governance.
- Planning levels.
- Governance and structure.

Entrepreneurial

This structure is built around the owner manager and is typical of small businesses in the early stages of development.

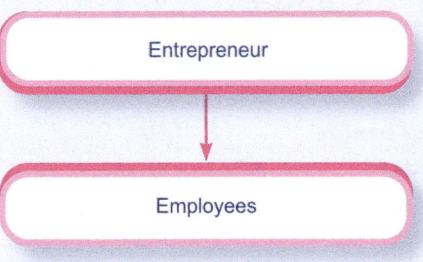

Advantages

- Fast decision making
- More responsive to market
- Goal congruence
- Good control
- Close bond to workforce

Disadvantages

- Lack of career structure
- Dependent on the capabilities of the manager/owner
- Cannot cope with diversification/growth

Functional/departmental structure

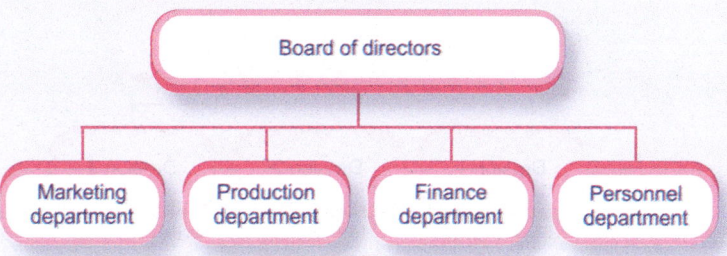

Advantages
- Economies of scale
- Standardisation
- Specialists more comfortable
- Career opportunities

Disadvantages
- Empire building
- Slow
- Conflicts between functions
- Cannot cope with diversification

Divisional/product structure

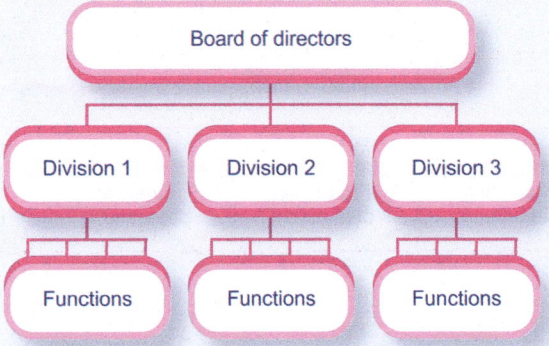

A **shared service approach** involves restructuring the provision of certain services within the organisation so that the service is centralised into one specific part of the organisation.

Divisions based on geographical areas

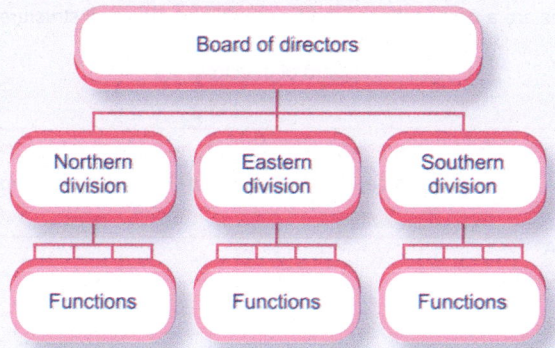

Advantages
- Enables growth
- Clear responsibility for products/ divisions
- Training of general managers
- Easily adapted for further diversification
- Top management free to concentrate on strategic matters

Disadvantages
- Potential loss of control
- Lack of goal congruence
- Duplication
- Specialists may feel isolated
- Allocation of central costs can be a problem

Matrix structure

Matrix structures are a combination of the functional and divisional structures.

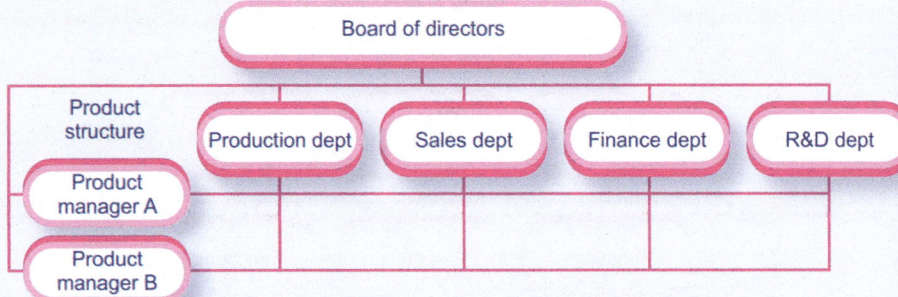

Advantages
- Advantages of both functional and divisional structures
- Flexibility
- Customer orientation
- Encourages teamwork and the exchange of opinions and expertise

Disadvantages
- Dual command and conflict
- Dilution of functional authority
- Time-consuming meetings
- Higher admin costs

Tall and flat organisations

Span of control

Scalar chain is the line of authority which can be traced up or down the chain of command from the most senior member of staff to the most junior. It relates to the number of levels of management within an organisation.

A manager's **span of control** is the number of people for whom he or she is directly responsible.

Factors that influence the span of control include:

- the nature of the work – the more repetitive or simple the work, the wider the span of control can be.
- the type of personnel – the more skilled and motivated the managers and the other staff members are, the wider the span of control can be.
- the location of personnel – if personnel are all located locally, it takes relatively little time and effort to supervise them. This allows the span of control to become wider.

Tall and flat organisations

A **tall organisation** has many levels of management (a long scalar chain and a narrow span of control).

A **flat organisation** has few levels of management (a short scalar chain and a wide span of control).

Governance

Governance refers to the authority structures, processes, and rules that an organisation has in place to determine how decisions get made, resources get allocated, and priorities get set.

Governance will therefore require the organisation to make decisions on the following areas:

- Specialisation: the extent to which an organisation's activities are divided into specialised roles.
- Standardisation: the degree to which an organisation operates under standard rules or procedures.
- Formalisation: the extent to which instructions and procedures are documented.
- Centralisation: the degree to which leaders at the top of the management hierarchy have authority to make certain decisions.
- Chain of command: the number of vertical levels or layers on the organisational chart (i.e. how tall the structure should be).
- Span of control: how wide or narrow this should be.

Centralisation and decentralisation

- In a centralised structure, the upper levels of an organisation's hierarchy retain the authority and make decisions.
- In a decentralised structure, the authority to take decisions is passed down to units and people at lower levels.

The factors that will affect the amount of decentralisation are:

- management style
- ability of management/employees
- geographic spread
- size of the organisation/scale of activities
- predictability of the environment.

Advantages of decentralisation

- Senior management free to concentrate on strategy.
- Better local decisions due to local expertise.
- Better motivation due to increased training and career path.
- Quicker responses/flexibility, due to smaller chain of command.

Disadvantages of decentralisation

- Loss of control by senior management.
- Dysfunctional decisions due to a lack of goal congruence.
- Poor decisions made by inexperienced managers.
- Training costs.
- Duplication of roles within the organisation.
- Extra costs in obtaining information.

Planning levels

Strategic planning

- Information predominantly environmental. Information imprecise and speculative.
- Long-term forecasts.
- Main output targets and plans.
- Ad hoc control system.

Management control

- Information concerned with efficiency and effective use of resources in the whole organisation.
- Information in financial and volume terms
- May involve responsibility centres.
- Includes measures of productivity, budget performance, labour and capacity utilisation.

Operational control

- Short-term control information.
- Very detailed.
- May be in terms of quantity, rates and times rather than finance.

Governance and structure

Different governance is likely to be applied to different structures.

Entrepreneurial structure		Divisional structure
Little	Specialisation	Lots
Little	Standardisation	Lots
Little	Formalisation	Lots
Very high	Centralisation	Very low
Flat	Chain of command	Tall
Wide	Span of control	Narrow

Organisational structure and governance

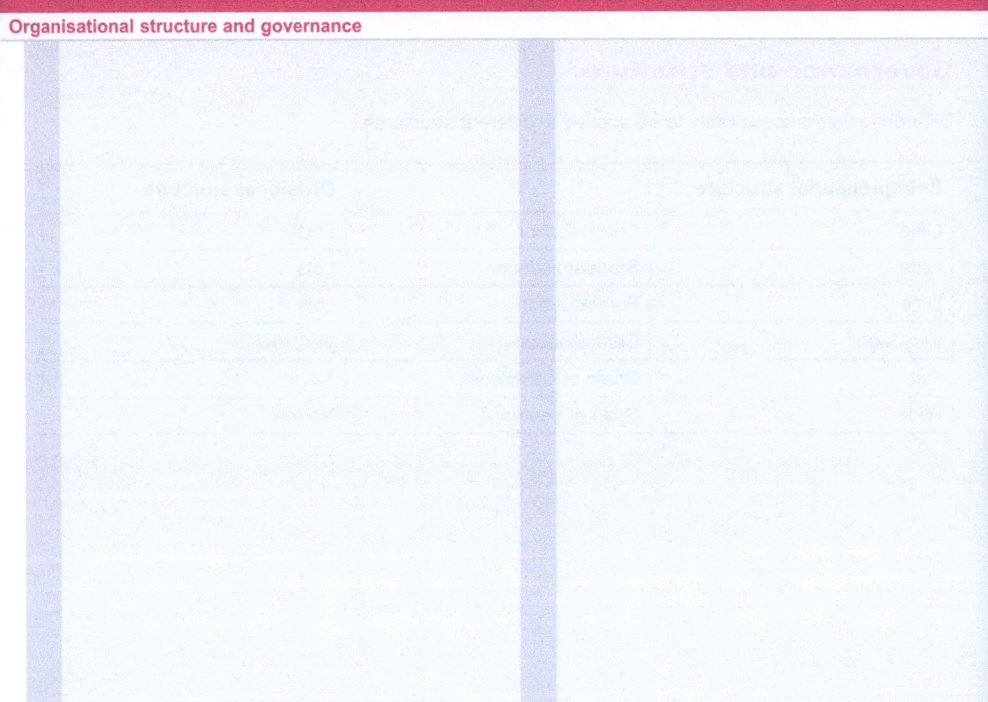

chapter 5

The role of the finance function

- Operations/production.
    - Sales and Marketing.
    - Human resources.
    - Finance.
    - IT.
    - Distribution and Logistics.

The role of the finance function

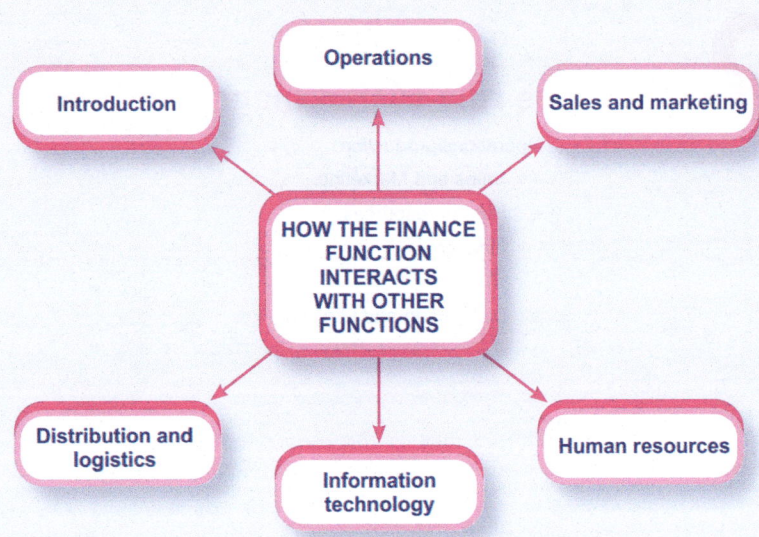

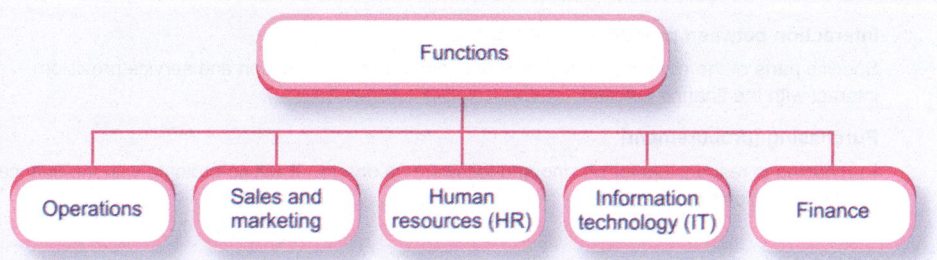

Operations/production

Interaction between production and finance

Specific parts of the organisation's operations (purchasing, production and service provision) interact with the finance function.

Purchasing (procurement)

Purchasing is responsible for placing and following up orders. It will co-ordinate with the finance function as follows:

Establishing credit terms	Finance will work with purchasing to negotiate credit terms with suppliers.
Prices	Finance will advise purchasing on the best price to pay suppliers.
Payment	Approved by purchasing and made by finance.
Data capture	Order details are input by purchasing and shared with finance.
Budgeting	Finance will consult with purchasing on the likely budget costs.

Production

The production of goods is a core part of the operations function. It liaises with the finance function as follows:

Costing	Finance will calculate production costs using information provided by operations.
Budgeting	Finance and operations will work together to determine the budgeted cost of production.
Cost v quality	Finance and operations will work together to establish the optimum balance between cost and quality.
Production process	Finance can assist in identifying inefficiencies in the production process (such as bottlenecks) and suggest improvements.
Inventory	Use various techniques to advise on stock levels and production required to meet demand.

The role of the finance function

Finance interaction with sales and marketing

The finance function will work with the sales and marketing function in the areas of:

Budgeting	Finance will discuss the likely sales volume with sales and marketing, in order to produce the sales budget.
Advertising	Finance will help set the budget and monitor the benefit generated.
Pricing	Finance will have an input into setting the optimum price.
Market share	Finance can provide sales volume information and help to determine market share.
Key Performance Indicators (KPIs)	Finance will help to establish and monitor the KPIs for sales and marketing.

Product/service development

Given the rapidly changing nature of the modern consumer's needs, effective product/service development is core to achieving or maintaining competitive advantage in the market.

With a sharp eye for the economic upside (or otherwise) the finance function will work collaboratively with sales and marketing to evaluate new product/service lines.

Interaction between HR and finance

- **Traditionally**, the HR function and the finance function worked independently. Finance viewed people as a cost whereas HR viewed them as an **asset**. Collaboration was limited, for example to establishing a budget for a reward programme.
- The **modern** approach is to view people as one of the **greatest assets** of the organisation and that finance and HR should work more closely with the 'people as assets' as their focus.
- Both functions have **overlapping responsibilities**, for example considering the costs and benefits of different HR policies.

Interaction between IT and finance

IT is one of the **greatest assets** of the organisation and that finance and IT should work more closely resulting in, for example:

- Smarter investment in IT.
- Improvements in information security and compliance.
- Improved data analytics.

The role of the finance function

SCM interaction with finance

- The role of the supply chain leader has become more prominent in recent years as the focus of SCM has moved away from cost reductions to creating a strategy that is aligned to the broader goals of the organisation.
- Meanwhile, the role of the finance function has been transformed. Finance now collaborates more closely with other functions; not just from a monitoring, reporting and risk management perspective, but also as supporters and enablers of performance.

chapter 6

Risk and risk management

- What is risk?
- Types of risk.
- Risk management.

Risk and risk management

What is risk?

> **Definition**
>
> Risk, in business, is the chance that future events or results may not be as expected. Risk can be quantified by assigning probabilities to various levels of loss.

Upside risks and downside risks

- Downside risk is the risk that results may be worse than expected.
- Upside risk is the risk that results may be better than expected.

The difference between risk and uncertainty

Risk is quantifiable; possible outcomes have associated probabilities and allow the use of mathematical techniques.

Uncertainty is unquantifiable, and the outcome cannot be mathematically modelled. It is difficult to incorporate uncertainty into decision making models.

Risk and return

Reasons why companies take risks include:

- To increase financial return – It is generally the case that firms must be willing to take higher risks if they want to achieve higher returns.
- To gain competitive advantage – To generate higher returns a business may have to take more risk in order to be competitive. Conversely, not accepting risk tends to make a business less dynamic and implies a 'follow the leader' strategy.

Investors may have different risk appetites. Some investors may be willing to take high risks whilst others prefer to seek only low risk opportunities. These different attitudes should be accepted and tolerated, and should not be the cause of prejudicial or discriminatory behaviour.

Types of risk

Business risk

This is the risk that the business fails. There are many sources of business risk such as:

- Strategic risk – the risk that the organisation's strategy (such as a strategy to enter a new overseas market) fails.
- Environmental risk – the risk that the organisation fails to adapt to changes in its environment (such as failing to adapt to new technology or new regulations).
- Product risk – the risk that the organisation's products fail (such as new products do not sell well or customers stop buying existing products).
- Market risk – the risk that the organisation fails to adapt to changes in its market (such as failing to react to new innovations by rivals or new rivals entering the market).

Operational risk

Definition

Operational risk refers to potential losses that might arise in business operations. It is 'the risk of losses resulting from inadequate or failed internal processes, people and systems, or external events' (Basel Committee on Banking Supervision).

Examples of operational risk are:

- Business disruption risk – this is the risk that the organisation's operations cannot continue to operate as normal.
- Regulatory risk – this is the risk that the business fails to meet regulatory standards or legislation.
- People risk – this is the risk of errors or problems caused by the people within the organisation.
- Process risk – this is the risk that processes are not efficient or fail.

Cyber risk

Definition

Cyber risk is a type of operational risk and is the risk of financial loss, disruption, or damage to an organisation caused by issues with the information technology systems they use.

- Malware – this is a term used to describe different types of malicious software, regardless of the purpose.
- Ransomware – software that prevents access to data until a ransom is paid.
- Botnets – networks of infected computers that are under the control of an attacker.
- Spyware – malware that is designed to spy on the victim and report back to the attacker.
- Trojans – legitimate software that secretly contains and releases malicious software onto a system.
- Malvertising – online advertising that has malicious software written into its code.
- Viruses – malware that replicates itself and spreads through programs, files and data.

Reputational risk

Definition

Reputation is the opinions people have and communicate about something, so reputational risk is the risk that people will have a negative opinion of an organisation and share that opinion with other people.

Reputation risk is for many organisations a down-side risk as the better the reputation of the business the more risk there is of losing that reputation.

There is a variety of considerations:

- Employees – the actions and behaviour of staff reflect the principles of the organisation they work for.
- Management – their position implies they are more likely to reflect the core values of the business, any digression is more significant.
- Accounting – any company found to be operating dubious accounting practices would lose confidence of customers and investors.
- Fraud – if a company allows fraud to take place, or does not allow appropriate action, it can lead to concerns from stakeholders.
- Bribery and corruption – if an organisation acts in an appropriate manner by offering or accepting bribery or any form of corruption this will damage their reputation.

Financial risk

Definition

Financial risk is the risk of change in a financial condition such as an exchange rate, interest rate, credit rating of a customer, or the price of goods.

Financial risks can come from a number of areas:

- Credit risk – the risk of non-payment by customers.
- Interest rate risk – the risk that interest rates change.
- Debt risk (gearing risk) – the risk that high levels of debt increase the risk of the business being bankrupt.

Risk management

The TARA framework

- Transfer – transfer risk wholly or in part to a third party e.g. by taking out insurance.
- Avoid – many risks are unavoidable, so the only choice here may be not to invest.
- Reduce – reduce or mitigate risks by limiting probability and/or impact, especially of downside exposure.
- Accept – accept the risk and deal with the consequences.

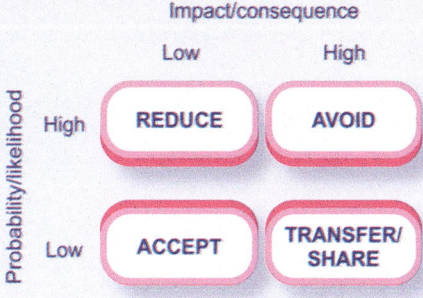

Risk and risk management

chapter 7

External analysis – the PESTLE model

- Political.
- Economic.
- Social.
- Technological.
- Legal.
- Environmental.

External analysis – the PESTLE model

EXTERNAL ANALYSIS – THE PESTLE MODEL

PESTLE Analysis of the macro environment

Political factors
- Taxation policy
- Government spending
- Foreign trade

Economic factors
- Economic growth
- Exchange/interest rates
- Inflation

Social factors
- Attitudes
- Demographics
- Income distribution

Technological factors
- New products
- Production methods
- Obsolescence

Legal factors
- Industry regulation
- Competition legislation
- Employment law

Environmental / ecological factors
- Sustainability
- Climate change
- Natural capital impact

chapter 8

The micro-economic environment

- Microeconomics.
- Demand.
- Supply.
- The price mechanism.
- Competition.

The micro-economic environment

Microeconomics

Part of an organisation's external PESTLE analysis will involve assessing the economic factors which will affect its industry. The key issue is to identify potential opportunities and threats.

Economics can be defined in various ways, including:

> 'the study of how society allocates scarce resources which have alternative uses, between competing ends'

It is useful to distinguish between two aspects of economics:

Microeconomics – the study of the economic behaviour of individual consumers, firms and industries.

Macroeconomics – considers aggregate behaviour, and the study of the sum of individual economic decisions – in other words, the workings of the economy as a whole.

Demand

Individual and market demand

Individual demand represents the amount that a consumer is willing and able to purchase at a given price – i.e. effective demand. Market demand shows the total amount of effective demand from all the consumers in a market.

Factors that shift the demand curve:

prices of other goods	Substitutes v complementary goods
income	Compare normal goods v inferior goods
taste/fashion	Could be influenced by advertising
other factors	Population size, credit terms

Changes in the price of the good/service do not shift the demand curve, they lead to an **expansion** or **contraction** along the curve.

This may be due to the **income effect** (as goods become more expensive, consumers can buy less of them), or the **substitution effect** (as goods become more expensive, consumers opt for cheaper alternatives)

As the price of a good rises, we expect demand for a normal good to fall, hence why the demand curve slopes **downwards**.

Supply

Supply is the amount that producers are willing and able to produce at a given price.

Factors that shift the supply curve

prices of other goods	Better to make them instead?
cost changes	e.g. new technology, greater efficiency, greater productivity, change in indirect taxes, e.g. VAT

Changes in the price of the good/service do not shift the supply curve, they lead to an **expansion** or **contraction** along the curve.

As the price of a good rises, we expect supply to rise, as suppliers are willing and able to produce more of it (due to the higher profits), hence why the supply curve slopes **upwards**.

Chapter 8

The price mechanism

Equilibrium price set by the interaction of supply and demand

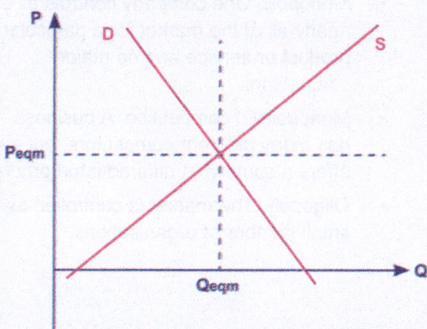

Price higher than equilibrium	Price lower than equilibrium
Excess supply – producers drop prices to clear surplus	Excess demand – shortages force prices up

Shifts in supply/demand

- Changes in supply/demand result in new equilibrium price.

- In exam questions consider whether it is the supply curve or the demand curve that is moving and in which direction.

- Example - for supply and demand of tea bags, a good tea harvest will reduce the cost of the tea leaves, making it cheaper to supply the product so the supply curve shifts outwards (S1 to S2). This increases the quantity sold to Q2 at a reduced price of P2.

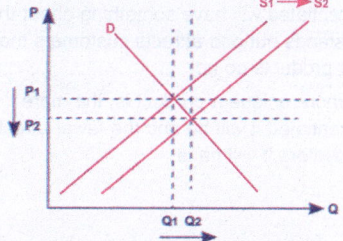

Competition

Healthy competition in a market benefits consumers. If competition is strong, with suppliers vying for the attention of customers, product / service quality will tend to rise and prices will be reasonable.

In this section, we look at various factors that determine the levels of competition for microeconomic markets.

Product features

Competition will be higher among products that are undifferentiated from their competitors' products. Those that are differentiated will have something about them that stands out and attracts customers that other products do not.

The more unique a product is, the more differentiated it will be and the fewer direct competitors it will have.

Number of sellers and buyers

Examples of markets where competition will be reduced are:

- Monopoly. One company controls all or nearly all of the market for a particular product or service and no major competitors.
- Monopolistic competition. A business has many different competitors, but each offers a somewhat differentiated product.
- Oligopoly. The market is controlled by a small number of organisations.

Barriers to entry

Barriers to entry are factors that make it difficult for a new entrant to gain an initial foothold in a market.

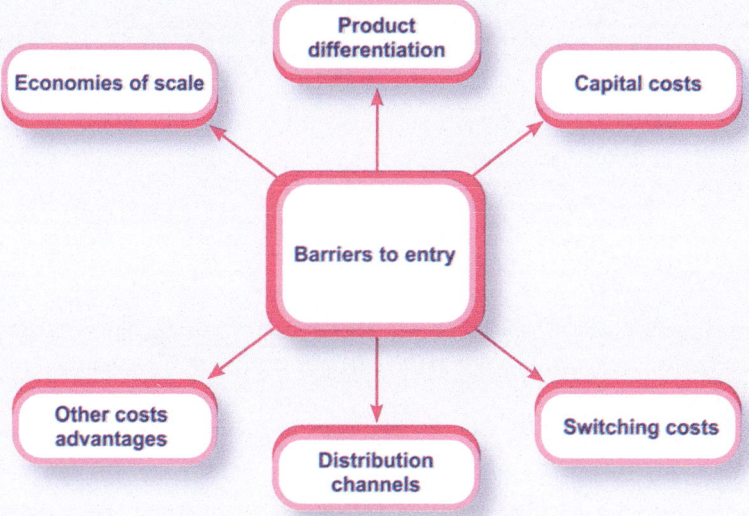

The micro-economic environment

chapter 9

Sustainability

- Benefits of acting sustainably.
- Sustainability and corporate social responsibility (CSR).
- Triple bottom line reporting (TBL).

Benefits of acting sustainably

Acting sustainably can contribute to the long-term success of the business and will help to maintain the well-being of the planet and people.

Benefits to stakeholders of the organisation include:

Stakeholder	Benefit
Workers/local community	Reduced waste and pollution will lead to a more pleasant, healthier environment. Guarantee of an appropriate minimum wage will lead to a better standard of living. Better workplace conditions will attract a higher calibre of workers and reduce accidents / injuries.
Customers	Many customers prefer dealing with businesses that follow sustainable policies such as looking after the environment or providing good working conditions and opportunities for workers, as they are seen as being more ethical.
Supply chain	Integrating sustainability into the supply chain will help suppliers achieve their own sustainability goals.
Shareholders	Shareholders look for an economically sound investment. Reduction of waste and increased efficiency can improve business profits. This could lead to higher long-term returns for investors.
Public	Businesses that are economically sound provide a stable job market for workers. Reduced pollution can lead to fewer environmental problems.

Three aspects of sustainable performance

It is important to note that sustainability is more than just looking at environmental concerns. It relates to three aspects:

- Environmental (planet).
- Social (people).
- Economic (profit) aspects of human society.

Some examples of unsustainable practices are:

Economic

- Underpayment of taxes – not contributing to maintaining the country's infrastructure (schools, roads, etc.).
- Bribery and corruption.

Social

- Rich companies exploiting third world labour as cheap manufacturing.

Environmental

- Long term damage to the environment from carbon dioxide and other greenhouse gases.

A key challenge is to ensure that organisations remain profitable while improving their environmental and social performance.

Sustainability affects every level of life, from the local neighbourhood to the entire planet.

> It is ethically wrong for this generation to benefit at the expense of future generations.

Sustainability and corporate social responsibility (CSR)

'CSR is the continuing commitment by business to behave ethically and contribute to economic development while improving the quality of life of the workforce and their families as well as of the local community and society at large.' (WBCSD meeting in The Netherlands, 1998).

Sustainability is thus one aspect of corporate social responsibility (CSR) and the two concepts are closely linked.

This is significant because many companies already have a commitment to CSR, setting targets and producing reports, for example. Calls for greater sustainability can thus be seen in the context of developing a firm's existing CSR policies and responsibilities, rather than something different and new.

Triple bottom line reporting (TBL)

- TBL accounting expands the traditional company reporting framework to take into account environmental and social performance in addition to financial/economic performance.
- Looks at reporting performance and decision making.
- The concept is also explained using the triple 'P' headings of 'People, Planet and Profit'.

Having a TBL perspective

A TBL business would attempt to do the following:

People

- Pay its workers fair wages.
- Maintain a safe working environment.
- Not use child labour or use suppliers who do.

- Promote the communities in which it operates.

Planet

- Reduce its 'ecological footprint'.
- Reduce energy usage.
- Limit environmental damage.
- Not be involved in resource depletion.

Profit

- Try to balance the profit objective with the other two elements of the TBL.

TBL thus attempts to show the full cost of any plans or development.

Once targets are set for these aspects and performance measured, then firms will incorporate the effects into decision making ('what gets measured gets done').

Sustainability

chapter 10

Professional ethics in accounting and business

- Fundamental Principles (IFAC Code of Ethics).
- Threats.
- Safeguards.

Professional ethics in accounting and business

Definition

Ethics can be defined as the 'moral principles that govern a person's behaviour or the conducting of an activity' (The Oxford English Dictionary).

Ethics is therefore concerned with

- Morality – the difference between right and wrong – 'doing the right thing'.
- How one should act in a certain situation.

Business ethics is simply the application of ethical principles to the problems typically encountered in a business setting.

What influences our ethical viewpoint?

Why should we bother with Ethics?

Possible advantages	Possible disadvantages
- To protect the public interest - To avoid discipline/fines - Improved reputation - Good ethics can attract customers - Good ethics can result in a more effective workforce - Ethics can give cost savings - Ethics can reduce risk	- Increased cost of sourcing materials from ethical sources - Lose profit by not trading with unethical customers/suppliers - Waste of management time?

Fundamental Principles (IFAC Code of Ethics)

The main advantages of a principles-based approach over a rules-based approach are that a principles-based approach is applicable to all situations, and gives individuals less chance of finding loopholes.

Integrity

- A professional accountant should be straightforward and honest in all professional and business relationships.
- Integrity also implies fair dealing and truthfulness.

Objectivity

- A professional accountant should not allow bias, conflict of interest or undue influence of others to override professional or business judgments.
- Need independence of mind and of appearance.

Professional competence

- A professional accountant has a continuing duty to maintain professional knowledge and skill at the level required to ensure that a client or employer receives competent professional service based on current developments in practice, legislation and techniques.
- A professional accountant should act diligently and in accordance with applicable technical and professional standards when providing professional services.

Confidentiality

- A professional accountant should respect the confidentiality of information acquired as a result of professional and business relationships and should not disclose any such information to third parties without proper and specific authority unless there is a legal or professional right or duty to disclose.

- Confidential information acquired as a result of professional and business relationships should not be used for the personal advantage of the professional accountant or third parties.

Professional behaviour

- A professional accountant should comply with relevant laws and regulations and should avoid any action that discredits the profession.

Threats

The self-interest threat

- May occur due to financial or other self-interest conflict
- e.g. fear of losing a client if you don't do what they ask.

The self-review threat

- May occur when previous judgement needs to be re-evaluated by the member responsible for that judgement
- e.g. doing accounts and then auditing them – would you admit to errors?

The advocacy threat

- May occur when a member promotes a position or opinion to the point that subsequent objectivity may be compromised
- e.g. arguing strongly with the tax office to try and reduce a client's tax bill – are you still being fair and truthful?

The familiarity or trust threat

- May occur when, because of a close or personal relationship, a member becomes too sympathetic to the interests of others
- e.g. having audited a client for 20 years do you fail to do enough testing as you trust them that the accounts are OK?

The intimidation threat

- May occur when a member may be deterred from acting objectively by threats, whether real or perceived
- e.g. Your employer or client may be very dominating or threatening so you just do whatever they say.

Safeguards

Safeguards are controls that mitigate, reduce or eliminate ethical threats

Two types:

- Safeguards created by the profession, legislation or regulation
    - e.g. CPD requirements, passing exams.
- Safeguards in the work environment.
    - e.g. policies dealing with receiving gifts, ethics policy, whistle blowing.

Businesses often incorporate the International Federation of Accountants (IFAC) principles into their own formal ethical codes.

chapter 11

Money laundering

- Money laundering offences.
- Dealing with suspected money laundering.
- Tipping off.
- Customer due diligence.
- Whistleblowing.

Money laundering

Definition

Money laundering is the process of exchanging criminally obtained money or other assets for clean money or other assets with no obvious link to the criminal origins. It is also the term for any money used to fund terrorism activities.

Money laundering involves 3 main stages:

1. Placement – where cash obtained through criminal activity is first placed into the financial system.
2. Layering – where the illegal cash is disguised by passing it through complex transactions making it difficult to trace.
3. Integration – where the illegally obtained funds are moved back into the legitimate economy and is now 'clean'.

Terrorist financing is fund raising, possessing or dealing with property or facilitating someone else to do so, when intending, knowing or suspecting or having reasonable cause to suspect that it is intended for the purposes of terrorism.

Terrorist property is money or property likely to be used for terrorist purposes or the proceeds of commissioning or carrying out terrorist acts.

Conviction of money laundering or terrorist financing is punishable by up to **14 years** imprisonment and/or an unlimited fine.

Money laundering offences

- Acquiring, possession or use of criminal property.
- Concealing or disguising or transferring criminal property, or removing it from the country.
- Failure to disclose knowledge or suspicion of money laundering (see next page for more details).
- Tipping off (see later for more details).

Failure to report knowledge or suspicion of money laundering

- Failure by an individual in the regulated sector to inform the Financial Intelligence Unit (FIU) or the firm's Money Laundering Reporting Officer (MLRO), as soon as practicable, of knowledge or suspicion that another person is engaged in money laundering, or
- Failure by MLROs in the regulated sector to make the required report to the FIU as soon as practicable if an internal report leads them to know or suspect that a person is engaged in money laundering.

If a member does not report known or suspected money laundering they can be charged with the offence of 'failure to report'. Confidentiality is not a defence.

If a business fails to meet its obligations under the Regulations, civil penalties or criminal sanctions can be imposed on the business and any individuals deemed responsible. This could include anyone in a senior position who neglected their own responsibilities or agreed to something that resulted in the compliance failure.

Dealing with suspected money laundering

Businesses, which are designed to assist in detecting money laundering and preventing the financial services organisations being used for money laundering purposes.

De minimis exceptions are **not** available in relation to either money laundering or terrorist financing offences – no amount is too trivial not to bother about.

At a minimum, an anti-money laundering program should incorporate:

- Money laundering and terrorist financing risk assessment.
- Implementation of systems, policies, controls and procedures that effectively manage the risk that the firm is exposed to in relation to money laundering activities and ensure compliance with the legislation, including:
  - Appointment of a Money Laundering Reporting Officer (MLRO).
  - Establishing internal reporting procedures to the MLRO.
  - Procedures for the reporting of suspicious transactions to the Financial Intelligence Unit (FIU).
  - Communication and training of all staff in the main requirements of the legislation.
  - Independent audit function to assess adequacy and effectiveness of the firm's procedures.
- Compliance with customer due diligence, enhanced due diligence and simplified due diligence requirements.
- Enhanced record keeping and data protection systems, policies and procedures.

Procedure for reporting known or suspected money laundering

There is no formal definition of suspicious. A suspicious transaction will often be inconsistent with the client's known or usual legitimate activities. Examples include:

- Unusually large cash deposits.
- Frequent exchanges of cash into other currencies.
- Overseas business arrangements with no clear business purpose.

It is a criminal offence not to report knowledge or suspicion of money laundering. Money laundering regulations require that:

- A person in the organisation is nominated to receive disclosures (usually an MLRO).
- Anyone in the organisation who suspects that a person is engaged in money laundering must disclose it to the MLRO.
- Where a disclosure is made to the MLRO, they must consider it in the light of any relevant information which is available to the organisation and determine whether it gives rise to suspicion.
- Where the MLRO does suspect money laundering, the information must be disclosed in a Suspicious Activity Report (SAR) to a regulatory body authorised for the purposes of these regulations (the FIU), such as the NCA in the UK.
- A SAR identifies:
  - Suspect's name, address, date of birth and nationality
  - Any identification or references seen
  - Nature of the activities giving rise to suspicion
  - Any other information that may be relevant i.e. the location of the laundered property, information held by the individual which identifies other parties involved in or connected to the matter.
- If there is no MLRO within the organisation then the SAR goes directly to the FIU (NCA in the UK).

Tipping off

Tipping off is telling the money laundering offender that the authorities have been informed or disclosing anything that might prejudice an investigation.

The penalty for this offence is a maximum of **two years** imprisonment, or an unlimited fine, or both.

A tipping off disclosure may be made in writing or verbally, and either directly or indirectly.

Customer due diligence

When considering any new client engagement, the professional accountant should assess the likelihood of money laundering.

Money Laundering Regulations 2017

Money laundering regulations state that Customer Due Diligence (CDD) must be applied in the following situations:

- When establishing a new business relationship.
- When carrying out an occasional transaction (i.e. involving £8,361, or the equivalent in Euros, or more).
- Where there is a suspicion of money laundering or terrorist financing.
- Where there are doubts about previously obtained customer identification information.
- At appropriate times, to existing clients, on a risk-sensitive basis.

If an organisation has a turnover of less than £100,000 (or the equivalent in Euros) they may be exempt as there is little risk of money laundering activity and to comply with the regulations would be an unnecessary burden.

When to apply Customer Due Diligence (CDD)

> CDD must be performed as soon as reasonably practical after contact is first made between the two parties. Where satisfactory evidence of identity is not obtained by the accountant, the business relationship or occasional transaction must not proceed any further.

Whistleblowing

Whistleblowing means disclosing information that a worker believes is evidence of illegality, gross waste, gross mismanagement, abuse of power, or substantial and specific danger to the public health and safety.

Many organisations (e.g. the NHS) have policies and procedures for 'internal' whistle blowing.

'External' whistle blowing could involve, for example, going to newspapers.

In the UK the Public Interest Disclosure Act 1998 protects you from dismissal by your employer provided you are acting in good faith.

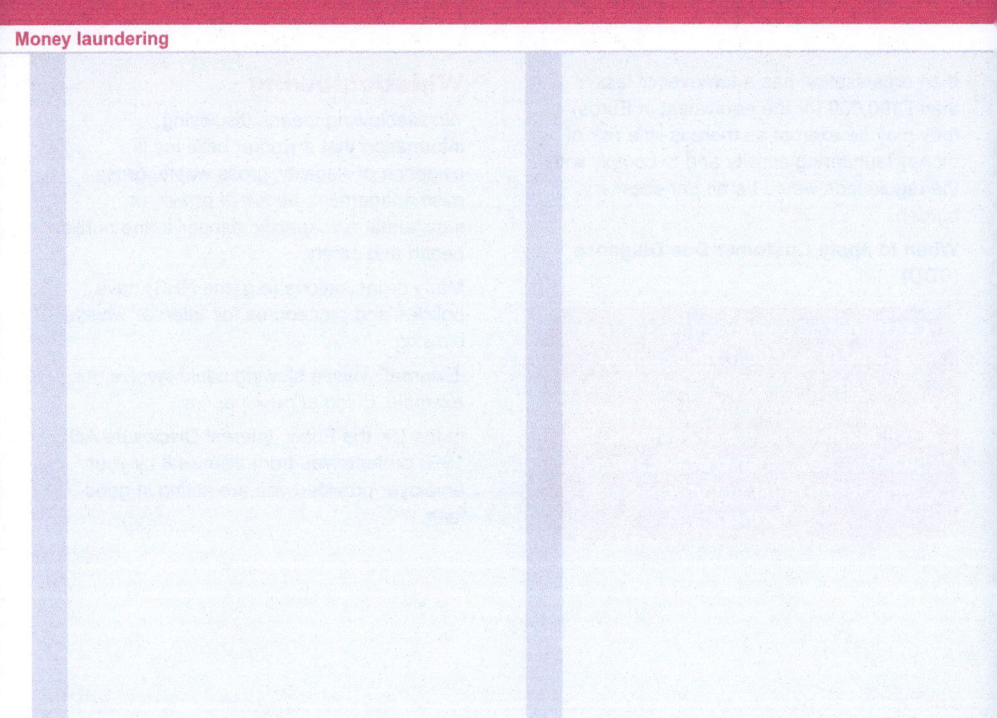

chapter 12

Technology affecting business and finance

- Offshoring/outsourcing.
- Cloud computing.
- Cloud accounting.
- The impact of emerging and developing technologies on accounting systems.

Repetitive tasks (for example, associated with the financial close and regulatory reporting and account reconciliation) are most likely to be automated, but developments in technology are allowing more **complex tasks** to be automated also.

Advantages

- Cost savings
- Focus on value adding activities
- Improved accuracy
- Positive return on investment
- Adaptability

Disadvantages

- Job/role uncertainty
- Relationship management
- IT staff competence required
- Training
- Change management

Finance professionals should not view automation as a threat but as an opportunity.

AI and machine learning

Artificial Intelligence is a system's ability to correctly interpret external data, to learn from such data, and to use those learnings to achieve specific goals and tasks through flexible adaptation.

This is often considered in the context of human-type robotics but reaches much further than this, and is set to transform the way we live and work.

Some of the more advanced activities and skills artificial intelligence can now master, and therefore present huge opportunities for developers and companies alike, include:

- Voice recognition
- Planning
- Learning
- Problem solving

Blockchain

A blockchain is a decentralised, distributed and public digital ledger that is used to record transactions across many computers. This means the record cannot be altered retroactively without the alteration of all subsequent blocks and the consensus of the network.

Key features of a blockchain:

- In a blockchain system, transactions are recorded by a number of participants using a network which operates via the internet.
- When a transaction takes place (for example, between a buyer and a seller) the details of that deal are recorded by everyone.
- The process of verifying the transaction is carried out by computers. This decentralised network of computers ensures that a single system cannot add new blocks to the chain.
- When a new block is added to a blockchain, it is linked to the previous block using a cryptographic hash (this turns data into a format that can only be read by authorised users) generated from the contents of the previous block.
- Blockchains and accounting.
- Ultimately, blockchain provides an unalterable, transparent record of all accountancy-related data.
- Examples of how blockchain can benefit the accounting profession include:
- Reducing the cost and of maintaining and reconciling ledgers.
- Providing absolute certainty over the ownership and history of assets, the existence of obligations and the measurement of amounts owed to a business and owed by a business.

- Freeing up time to allow staff to concentrate on other responsibilities such as planning, valuation, reporting etc., rather than record-keeping.

Electronic filing of documents

An electronic file management system is a good option for a variety of businesses across a number of different industries. Government agencies, medical practices, insurance companies, legal firms, finance functions and highly technical industries may all benefit from an electronic file management system.

Documentation previously stored on paper (or some physical format), becomes more valuable and easier to use when translated into an electronic format.

Benefits

- Reliable backup assistance and disaster recovery methods.
- Accurate, organised electronic databases.
- Instant, 24/7 access, no matter where the user is located.
- Increased workplace productivity.
- Enhanced customer service.

Disadvantages

- A sizeable initial set up cost for the system.
- The need to keep hardware and software up to date.
- Data security and the risk of data breaches.

Electronic signing of documents

Electronic signatures deliver a way to sign documents in the online world, much like one signs a document with a pen in the offline world.

Electronic signatures come in many forms, including:

- Typewritten.
- Scanned.
- An electronic representation of a handwritten signature.
- A unique representation of characters.
- A digital representation of characteristics, for example, fingerprint or retina scan.
- A signature created by cryptographic means.

Data analytics

Data analytics is the process of collecting, organising and analysing large sets of data (big data) to discover patterns and other information which an organisation can use to inform future decisions.

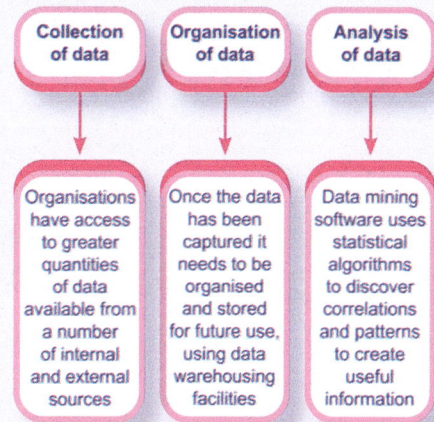

Collection of data	Organisation of data	Analysis of data
Organisations have access to greater quantities of data available from a number of internal and external sources	Once the data has been captured it needs to be organised and stored for future use, using data warehousing facilities	Data mining software uses statistical algorithms to discover correlations and patterns to create useful information

Technology affecting business and finance

Benefits

- Fresh insight and understanding
- Performance improvement
- Market segmentation and customisation
- Decision making
- Innovation
- Risk management

Offshoring/outsourcing

Definition

Offshoring refers to the process of outsourcing or relocating some of an organisation's functions from one country to another, usually in an effort to reduce costs.

Offshoring would not have been possible without the improvements in technology that allowed seamless communication between customers and business functions in locations across the world.

Benefits of offshoring:

- Cost savings

Disadvantages of offshoring:

- Cultural differences and language barriers

Outsourcing

Definition

Outsourcing means contracting out aspects of the work of the organisation previously done in-house, to specialist providers.

An organisation will often outsource its non-core services to a third party, allowing them to focus on their core competencies which are integral to the organisation's ability to create and to add value.

Benefits of outsourcing:

- Staff are freed up to focus on value adding activities to gain competitive advantage.
- The cost structure of the business will change, allowing cost savings to be achieved.
- Improved productivity as the outsourced work is now being done by experts who may also use automation.
- Supplier expertise can also lead to improved accuracy and adherence to regulations.

Disadvantages of outsourcing:

- Cost issues – the supplier will want to make a profit margin.
- Loss of core competence.
- Transaction costs.
- Finality of decision.
- Risk of loss of confidential information.
- Risk of continuity of supply if the supplier has problems.
- Difficulty agreeing/enforcing contract terms.
- Damage to employee morale if redundancies occur or if organisational culture is eroded.

Cloud computing

> **Definition**
>
> **Cloud computing** is the delivery of on-demand computing resources – everything from applications to data centres – over the internet. (IBM).

The basic idea and application of cloud computing sees users log in to an account in order to access, manage and process files and software via remote servers hosted on the internet. This replaces the traditional method of owning and running software locally on a computer or networked server.

Advantages

- Flexibility and scalability
- Cost efficient
- Security
- Flexible working
- Environment

Disadvantages

- Organisational change
- Contract management
- Security, privacy and compliance
- Reliance

Cloud accounting

Definition

Cloud accounting is a system whereby users subscribe to an online accounting software solution and move their books to the cloud. Cloud accounting software holds accounts data remotely on secure servers (not onsite on the company's computers).

Benefits

- Access to real-time financial performance and position information.
- Multi-user access for online collaboration: cloud accounting enables access to large networks.
- Nothing to install or update, automatic backup.
- More apps and plug-ins are available.
- Access levels can be controlled.
- Security and privacy should be airtight.
- Access from any location with an internet connection.
- Software updates delivered faster and more easily by cloud provider.

Disadvantages

- Users' ability to connect depends on internet connection.
- Supplier's ability to adhere to data protection regulations will be crucial.
- May become difficult to switch providers/systems.

The impact of emerging and developing technologies on accounting systems

- Process automation and the use of AI and machine learning can provide opportunities for finance teams to automate repetitive work and concentrate on adding value to the business.
- The use of blockchain technology along with electronic filing and signing can add security and integrity to transactions and documents.

Offshoring/outsourcing

- Technological advantages have made these possible.
- The use of offshoring and outsourcing leads to changes in a business's cost structure, allows it to access new markets and to operate from anywhere.

Cloud accounting

- Cloud computing involves accessing software and data over the internet rather than from an office based server.
- Cloud accounting offers flexibility but businesses must be aware of its risks.

chapter 13

Data protection, information security and cybersecurity

- GDPR.
- Cybersecurity.

GDPR

Legislation which details the following principles about data:

- Used fairly, lawfully and transparently.
- Used for specified, explicit purposes (Purpose limitation).
- Used in a way that is adequate, relevant and limited to only what is necessary.
- Accurate and, where required, kept up to date.
- Kept for no longer than is necessary (storage limitation).
- Handled in a way that ensures appropriate security.
- Accountability – ability to prove that the regulations are being complied with.

Data protection breaches

As the business world becomes more complex, organisations are holding increasing amounts of data about individuals.

Data protection is concerned with protecting individuals against the misuse of this information.

If an organisation fails to comply with the GDPR, it can be fined.

EU maximum fines – the higher of €20 million or 4% of annual global turnover.

UK maximum fines – the higher of £17.5 million or 4% of annual global turnover.

Requirements:

- Report a breach to the relevant supervisory authority within 72 hours of becoming aware of the breach, where feasible.
- If the breach is likely to result in a high risk of adversely affecting individuals' rights and freedoms, the organisation

must also inform those individuals without undue delay.

- Organisations should ensure that they have robust breach detection, investigation and internal reporting procedures in place, in order to facilitate decision-making about whether or not there is a need to notify the relevant supervisory authority or the affected individuals, or both.
- Records must be kept of any personal data breaches, regardless of whether notification to the authorities or the individuals concerned is required.

Cybersecurity

Definition

Cyber security is the protection of internet-connected systems, including hardware, software and data, from cyber attacks.

A **cyber attack** is a malicious and deliberate attempt by an individual or organisation to breach the information system of another individual or organisation.

Data protection, information security and cybersecurity

Key risks of cyber attacks

Risk	Description
Malware	Software designed to cause damage to a single computer, server or computer network. Worms, viruses and trojans are all varieties of malware, distinguished from one another by the means by which they reproduce and spread. These attacks may render a computer or network inoperable, or grant the attacker access so that they can control the system remotely.
Phishing	Cybercriminals craft emails to fool a target into taking some harmful action. The recipient might be tricked into downloading malware that is disguised as an important document or urged to click on a link that takes them to a fake website where they will be asked for sensitive information like usernames and password.
Denial of service	A brute force method to try to stop an online service from working properly.
Man in the middle	Attackers manage to interpose themselves secretly between the user and a web service that they are trying to access.

Chapter 14

Information and Big Data

- Information.
- Big Data.

Information

Definition

Data consists of numbers, letters, symbols, raw facts, events and transactions which have been recorded but not yet processed into a form that is suitable for making decisions.

Information is data that has been processed in such a way that is has a meaning to the person that receives it, who may then use it to improve the quality of decision-making.

Information is a vital requirement within any business and is required both internally and externally.

Characteristics of good information

Good information should be:

Accurate

Complete

Cost effective

Understandable

Relevant

Authoritative

Timely

Easy to use

Big data

Definition

Big Data is a term for a collection of data which is so large it becomes difficult to store and process using traditional databases and data processing applications.

The five V's: represent the defining characteristics of Big Data:

- **Velocity**: Data is now streaming from sources such as social media sites at a virtually constant rate and current processing servers are unable to cope with this flow and generate meaningful real-time analysis.
- **Volume**: More sources of data and an increase in data generation in the digital age combine to increase the volume of data to a potentially unmanageable level.
- **Variety**: Traditionally data was structured and in similar and consistent formats such as Excel spreadsheets and standard databases. Data can now be generated and collected in a huge range of formats including rich text, audio and GPS data amongst others.
- **Veracity**: Because of so many different sources there is an increased risk of inaccuracies.
- **Value**: Once businesses have the data it needs to be used in a way that adds value.

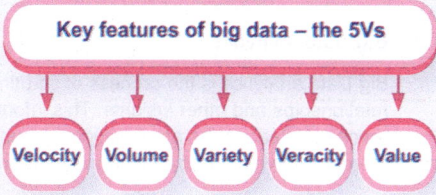

Key features of big data – the 5Vs

Velocity | Volume | Variety | Veracity | Value

Information and Big Data

Benefits of Big Data	Risks associated with Big Data
- Drives innovation – can be used to develop the next generation of products or services - Improves customer service and decision making - Can create new revenue streams - Source of competitive advantage - Ensures measurable outcomes	- Skills to use systems may not exist - Security of data - Valuable time may be spent measuring relationships that have no organisational value - Incorrect data may result in incorrect conclusions - Technical difficulties integrating systems - Cost of establishing hardware and software

Big Data analytics

Big Data analytics is the process of scrutinising Big Data to identify patterns, correlations, relationships and other insights. This information can inform decision making and have a wide reaching effect on the organisation's competitive strategy and marketing campaigns. It can therefore have a direct impact on future profitability.

chapter 15

Visualising information

- Methods of communication.
- Good communication.
- Using tables.
- Using images.
- Using IT.

Visualising information

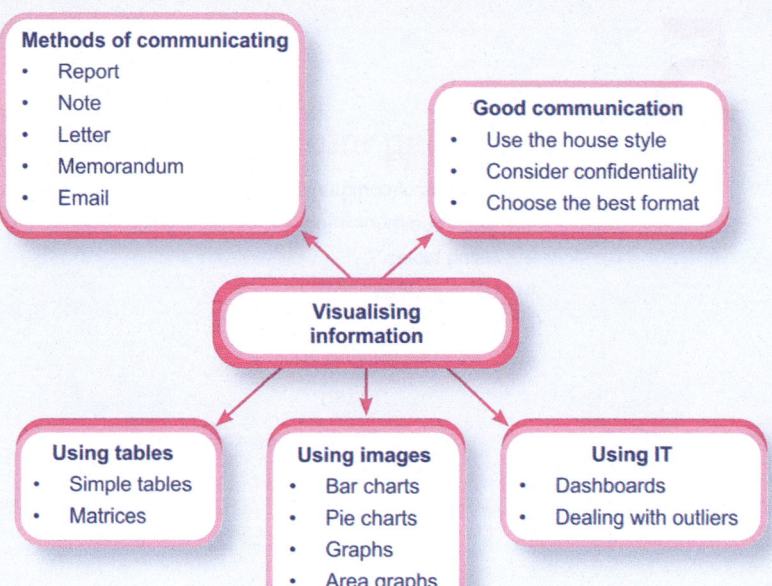

Index

Index

A
Artificial Intelligence 90

B
Barriers to entry 67
Big Data 105
Big Data analytics 106
Blockchain 91
Blockchain technology 98

C
Chairman 18
Characteristics of good information 104
Charities 12
Cloud accounting 97, 98
Cloud computing 96
Clubs 7
Commercial companies 7
Companies House 17
Competition 66
Confidentiality 78
Conflicts 27
Connected 24, 26
Cooperatives 7
Corporate social responsibility 72
CSR 72
Customer due diligence 86, 87
Cyber attack 101
Cyber security 101

D
Data 104
Data analytics 93
Data protection breaches 100
Debt 13
Denial of service 102
Directors 16, 18
Directors duties 19

E
Electronic filing of documents 92
Electronic signing of documents 93
Entrepreneurial 32
Equilibrium 65
Equity 13
Ethics 77
Executive director 18
External 24, 26

Index

F
Fair value 21
Financial Conduct Authority (FCA) 17
Firm 20

G
GDPR 100
General partnership 20
Goodwill 21

I
IFAC code of ethics 78
Information 104
Integration 82
Integrity 78
Internal 24, 26

J
Joint and several 21

L
Layering 82
Limited liability companies 8

M
Malware 102
Managing director 18
Man in the middle 102
Mendelow's 28
Money laundering 81, 82
Money laundering offences 83
Monopolistic competition 66
Monopoly 66

N
Non-executive director 18
Not-for-profit 7
Not-for-profit organisations (NFPs) 7, 9

O
Objectivity 78
Offshoring 94
Oligopoly 66
Organisational types 7
Organisations 6
Outsourcing 95
Ownership/control 7

Index

P

Partnership 20
Partnerships 7
People 71
Phishing 102
Placement 82
Planet 71
Primary 24
Private sector 7, 10, 12
Private sector limited liability 7
Process automation 98
Professional behaviour 79
Professional competence 78
Profit 5, 9, 15, 17, 71
Profit orientation 7
Profit-seeking 7
Public sector 7, 10

R

Repetitive tasks 90
Risk averse 24
Risk neutral 24
Risk seeking 24
Robotics 90

S

Safeguards 80
Secondary 24
Separation of ownership and control 12
Services vs. manufacuring organisations 11
Shareholders 16, 20, 70
Shifts in supply 65
Social needs 7
Sole traders 8
Stakeholders 25
Sustainability 69

T

TBL 72, 73
The advocacy threat 79
The familiarity or trust threat 80
The intimidation threat 80
The price mechanism 65
The self-interest threat 79
The self-review threat 79
Threats 79
Tipping off 86
Triple bottom line reporting 72
Types of funding 12

U

Unlimited liability partnerships 16, 20

V

Variety 105
Velocity 105
Veracity 105
Visualising information 108
Volume 105

W

Whistleblowing 87

Index